The operations of the French fleet under the Count de Grasse in 1781-2.

John Gilmary Shea

Bradford Club Series.

NUMBER THREE.

LE COMTE DE GRASSE

THE

OPERATIONS

OF

THE FRENCH FLEET

UNDER THE

Count De Grasse

IN 1781-2

AS DESCRIBED IN TWO CONTEMPORANEOUS JOURNALS

NEW YORK
MDCCCLXIV

Entered according to an Act of Congress, in the year 1864,
By John B. Moreau,
FOR THE BRADFORD CLUB,
in the Clerk's Office of the District Court of the United States
for the Southern District of New York

ONE HUNDRED AND FIFTY COPIES PRINTED

SUBSCRIBER'S COPY.

No

THE BRADFORD CLUB.

Under this designation, a few gentlemen interested in the study of American History and Literature, propose occasionally to print limited editions of such manuscripts and scarce pamphlets as may be deemed of value towards illustrating these subjects. They will seek to obtain, for this purpose, unpublished journals or correspondence containing matter worthy of record, and which may not properly be included in the Historical Collections or Documentary Histories of the several states. Such unpretending cotemporary chronicles often throw precious light upon the motives of action, and the imperfectly narrated events of by-gone days, perhaps briefly touched upon in dry official documents.

The Club may also issue fac-similes of curious manuscripts, or documents worthy of notice, which like the printed issues will bear its imprint.

"These are the
Registers, the chronicles of the age
They were written in, and speak the truth of History
Better than a hundred of your printed
Communications."—*Shakerly Marmyon's Antiquary*

William Bradford, the first New York Printer, whose name they have adopted, came to this country in 1682, and established his press in the neighborhood of Philadelphia. In 1693 he removed to this city, and set up the first press "at the sign of the Bible." His first work, printed in this colony, was entitled "The Laws and Acts of the

General Assembly." During a period of thirty years, he was the only Printer in the Province, and in his imprints, he styled himself "Printer to the King." In 1725 he printed our first newspaper, *The New York Gazette*. He continued the business of his profession until within a few years of his death, which occurred in 1752, at the age of 92 years. He was described in an obituary notice of the day as "a man of great sobriety and industry, a real friend to the poor and needy, and kind and affable to all."

April, 1859.

PREFACE.

The Bradford Club having received from one of the members, Mr J. C. Brevoort of Brooklyn, a very neatly written manuscript, comprising a journal of an officer in the fleet of the Count de Grasse in 1781-82, believed that it would form a most appropriate volume, as portraying the naval operations of France during the Revolution, and especially of that fleet which rendered such timely service to our cause by its aid in the siege of Yorktown and in the repulse of Graves off the Chesapeake

The manuscript bears the name of the Chevalier de Goussencourt, and the first question of course was, in what capacity he served Although through the kindness of my excellent and now deceased friend, Mr Henry de Courcy, whose family has been for nearly two centuries well represented in the French navy, I had more than usual opportunity for pursuing the investigation, our researches have been futile The only indication as to his vessel is in the fact that he returned to France in the squadron composed of the Languedoc, 80, Baron Daross, the Diadême, 74, de Montéclerc, and the Magnanime, 74, le Begue He bestows great praise on Montéclerc for his services after the fight, and defends the conduct of Daross during it Mr de Courcy accordingly applied to the navy department in Paris with this guide. he found the rolls of de Grasse's fleet complete, but received from the archivist who made a regular search, the following report

" No officer of the name of Goussencourt was on the expedition of

PREFACE.

Admiral de Grasse in 1782. An examination just made of the rolls of the Languedoc, Diademe and Magnanime has afforded no result, except that of establishing perfectly that no name exists there which bears the remotest resemblance to that of Goussencourt. The same is true of the navy lists from 1781 to 1787."

Mr. de Courcy's inquiries among the aged naval officers of France were as fruitless.

It would appear that the name was a pseudonyme, and such was the opinion of the navy bureau, but as he might have belonged to the army, Mr. de Courcy endeavored to find whether any member of the de Goussencourt family, though bearing another name, served on the fleet; but though he discovered a living general of the name, was unable to obtain any satisfactory information.

De Goussencourt is hostile to the Count de Grasse, and very freely canvasses his operations. Fortunately there exists another journal printed nominally at Amsterdam in 1782, written in the interest of that commander, and, perhaps from his hand. It is anonymous, and the vessel on which the writer served is also left an impenetrable secret. This is also here presented, that the two versions may be confronted, and the reader be better enabled to judge of the whole campaign.

A third French account, not of the whole expedition, but of the fatal battle with Rodney, is contained in the anonymous "Voyage d'un Suisse dans différentes colonies d'Amerique pendant la derniere Guerre" Neuchatel, 1786. The writer was on one of the French vessels that escaped from the battle, but like the other writings, carefully avoids mentioning its name or giving us any clue to it.

This account, with Rodney's despatches, give all the accessible reports.

I have given such notices of the French officers mentioned as I could glean here or get from my good friends in France. As to Admiral de Grasse himself, the family, as it will be seen, have given me their aid in compiling the sketch of his life.

J. G. SHEA.

INTRODUCTION.

The present war, in which some of our sister states forming a new confederacy are attempting alike the establishment of a national existence and conquest of other portions of our territory, shows the immense advantage enjoyed in such a war by the party possessing a power on the ocean. The American government has never, so to say, had a navy. A gallant nucleus of a maritime army has indeed won renown, but our vessels are too few in number, and inadequate in force and armament to be at all commensurate with our dignity as one of the great powers of the world, or even with the protection of our mercantile marine and the seacoast of our land, which in its length would form no inconsiderable part of the earth's circumference No American fleet ever sailed forth able to cope successfully with fleets such as England, France, Holland, and Spain, have had on the ocean in successive wars.

The revolted states have no navy, and no means of fitting one out. From a variety of causes they can neither build nor man vessels, and the so-called privateers of the Southern confederacy, few in number, are really English vessels, built and equipped in England, under the countenance, if not by the direct aid, of the English government, and often commanded by British subjects.

Inadequate therefore as the American navy is, it has nevertheless contributed immensely to the strength of government in its operations at Hatteras, Port Royal, Pensacola, Charleston, New Orleans, as well as on the Mississippi and other rivers, besides the great advantage it affords of rapid and unmolested transportation of troops from one extremity to the other.

We are thus enabled, by our actual reference to day, to estimate more justly the importance of the French naval operations on the Atlantic in the last century, on the ultimate result of our Revolutionary struggle, by actual aid in military operations, by defeating those of the enemy, or rendering them safe only when convoyed by powerful fleets. It was to us, what in the present war, an open alliance between England and the revolted states would be to them. The damage caused by the British privateers has been great, but a declaration of war by England or France against us would entail on our part the armament of fleets such as our country has never witnessed, and which, notwithstanding the immense expenses government should prepare at once, and not leave to the eventuality of diplomatic complications, or the good faith of nations, whom the history of the past should teach us not to trust too implicitly.

In turning our gaze to the period of our early struggle for nationhood, we find the period, one especially calling out naval operations.

The French, whose loss of their vast American possessions still rankled in their bosoms, beheld with undisguised exultation the outburst in the ancient colonies of England, which their statesmen had foreseen, and which in its certain future, as the sure result of the conquest of Canada, consoled them for its loss. Her ports gladly sheltered those daring American privateers, whose exploits carried terror through English commerce. Ere long too, arms, money and experienced officers reached America from France; among the last, that De Kalb, who secretly traversing the country years before, had clearly discerned the coming revolution with which his name was to be indissolubly connected.

The government of France stood ostensibly neutral between England and her colonies, but in reality was preparing for a war which gratified every instinct of a French heart. The navy, neglected during the close of the disgraceful reign of Louis XV, had, under the young monarch, been increased in number, strength and morale, and the officers burned with a desire to engage their hated rivals on the ocean, and at last gain that mastery on water which England had so long possessed

France had never been equal to England at sea, and on the decline of Spanish and Dutch naval strength, Britain stood alone; many considerations combining to compel her to sacrifice all to maintain the power she had acquired. To effect this, all the conquests of science were immediately utilized: no improvement in naval architecture, in ordnance or navigation, was overlooked, the parasites of the court banished from the navy, and the commands filled by capable and thoroughly educated seamen, before whom the fate of Byng stood as the stern sentence of public opinion on defeat.

Yet never, perhaps, till our day, was France so nearly a match for England as at the period of which we speak. Brest and Toulon had been active in fitting out her ships of the line and frigates, but though her officers were in many cases men of scientific training, science and progress had been overlooked, and the aristocratic element possessed undisputed the whole service. No one could become a midshipman or ensign without presenting his fourteen quarterings, showing his indisputable right to be reckoned among the noblesse. Two facts will show their lack of progress. The coppering of vessels had been adopted by the English, and though one of the most capable officers in France urged upon the government the advantage which would result from the use of sheathing, his advice was unheeded; and France began this war with this great disadvantage of fighting the swift copper-fastened men-of-war of her rival with her own old fashioned wooden bottoms. The custom of preparing for action on only one side of the ship had been abandoned by the English, but retained by the French, and it more than once occurred that an English vessel by a slight manœuvre was able to pour into the unprepared side of a French vessel a broadside which could not be returned.

Yet France, regardless as she then was of such advantages, was eager for the struggle, and the navy especially hailed the gathering cloud of war with exultation.

When the French government, at last, resolved to take an active part in the war, a fleet under Charles Henry Count d'Estaing, was sent out from Toulon on the 13th of April, 1778, with orders to attack any fleet bound to or from America; and at the same time they prepared to send out another fleet from Brest, under Count d'Orvilliers. The first hostility took place off the coasts of Brittany, the Arethusa, 26, of Keppel's fleet, having on the 17th of June begun the war by attacking the Belle Poule, a French vessel of equal force, commanded by the brave La Clocheterie, who signalized himself in the first, to die fighting most gallantly in the last battle of the war. This led to a fiercely contested, but indecisive action off Ushant, on the 21st July 1778, between the English fleet under Keppel, and the French fleet under the Count d'Orvilliers.

Mean while the Count d'Estaing ran across the

Atlantic and began hostilities on the 30th June, by capturing an English vessel off Bermuda. On the 5th of the next month, the frigate Engageante of his fleet took the English frigate Rose, the first real capture in the war. An unfortunate delay prevented his blockading Howe in the Delaware, and he appeared off Sandy Hook July 11, to be abandoned by pilots, and outgeneraled by Howe, who made such an appearance of force in New York bay with a lot of miserable hulks, that he prevented d'Estaing, misled too by tory pilots, from entering, when he might in fact have sailed up to the city and closed the war. D'Estaing then concerted a plan with Lafayette and Sullivan to take Rhode Island. He ran into Newport and compelled the English to destroy their vessels there. Just as operations were about to begin, Howe appeared, d'Estaing went out to meet him, Howe avoided an action, a storm came on, d'Estaing's fleet suffered, and abandoning the siege of Newport to the great dissatisfaction of Sullivan, he sailed to Boston to repair.

Leaving Boston he allowed Hotham's squadron from New York to go almost before his eyes to Barbadoes. Proceeding to Guadaloupe, in December he engaged Barrington, but failed to capture his small squadron, and saw his arms repulsed with loss in his attack on St. Lucia, Dec. 18.

The next year, having been reinforced by four vessels under de Grasse, he reduced the islands of Saint Martin, St. Bartholomew, and St. Vincent. On the last day of June, he sailed from Fort Royal with twenty-five vessels of the line, and two frigates, and early in July, after a sharp action, reduced Granada. On the 6th, a very sharp engagement took place between d'Estaing and Byron, in which the latter suffered severely.

The next operation of Count d'Estaing was another attack on an English post in the United States. Savannah was assailed on the 9th of October, by American and French troops, the former under Lincoln, the latter led by d'Estaing in person; but in spite of the valor of the allies, they were repulsed with heavy loss. This ended the naval and military campaign of d'Estaing, from which the Americans had expected much and obtained nothing.

The Count de Guichen, who succeeded to the command of the French fleet in the West Indies, brought Rodney to action, April 17, 1780, but the battle produced no result, and a similarly indecisive action took place May 19.

In 1781, the Chevalier Destouches sent a part of his fleet from Boston to the Chesapeake, under M de Tilly, who captured the Romulus, 44 guns, and several transports, but most of the enemy's vessels ran up to Portsmouth. Destouches himself then sailed to the Chesapeake, and had a spirited action with Graves, in which he put three of the English vessels hors de combat De Ternay, who brought another French squadron across the Atlantic, allowed an English squadron to escape from him, and died of mortification soon after his arrival.

Such had been the main operations of the French navy in American waters up to the time of the campaign of the Count de Grasse, described in these pages. That such fleets were sent by both governments to operate in the dangerous waters of the West Indian Archipelago, and waste their strength on the reduction of petty islands, when a continent was at stake, is not easily explained. The time was spent in taking and retaking small and unimportant isles, the possession of which was of no strategic importance. In the war on the Continent, the operations at Newport and Savannah, both entire failures, and the operations of Destouches in the Chesapeake, alone show the intervention of our transatlantic allies, and thus far, it is clear, that the assistance rendered by the French navy had been of little moment, except in the fact that it gave occupation to all England's fleets.

Of the career of the Count de Grasse, whose last fatal battle in a manner closed the war, we need not enter here. The journals give the details in full.

FRANCIS JOSEPH PAUL DE GRASSE-ROUVILLE, COUNT DE GRASSE, MARQUIS DE TILLY, LIEUTENANT-GENERAL DES ARMÉES NAVALES.

Though not regarded in France as one of the glories of the French navy, in consequence of the disaster which closed his naval career, the name of De Grasse is associated in the American mind with the ultimate triumph of national independence, and popular gratitude rewards his exertions and sacrifices by its lasting reverence. The family from which he sprung was one of the oldest of the French noblesse, claiming descent from Rodoard, Prince of Antibes in 993, and boasting of its alliance by intermarriage with the royal houses of France, Spain, and Sicily. The Captal de Buch, so famous in Froissart, was one of the ancestors of the Count de Grasse. His family bore the name of de Grasse from the eleventh century, and that of Rouville from 1676.

His father, François de Grasse-Rouville, Marquis de Grasse, was a captain in the army, but two of his sons, Joseph de Grasse, a knight of Malta, who served at Louisbourg, and was a captain in 1757, and François Joseph Paul, sought the guerdon of their ambition in the naval career.

François Joseph Paul was born in 1723; but of his earlier career, even the biography published by his son affords us no particulars. At the commencement of the war with England, brought on by the American Revolution, he was captain of the Robuste, 74, and had been in active service, apparently in her since 1775. With that vessel he took an active part in the naval engagement fought off Ouessant in July, 1778. In the following year, still in the same vessel, he sailed as *chef-d'escadre*, or commodore, from Brest, with four ships of the line, and anchored in the road of Fort Royal, February 20, 1779. He shared in the triumphs and reverses of d'Estaing's campaign, in the reduction of Granada, in the siege of Savannah, and after which he sailed to the West Indies with a portion of the fleet. Here he distinguished himself in 1780, under de Guichen, in his engagements with Rodney, rescuing the Sphynx and Artesien from a superior English force. Declining the command of the squadron on the ground of health, he returned to France, where he was raised by the king to the rank of lieutenant-general or admiral, and invested with the command of the fleet in the West Indies, which d'Estaing and de Guichen had hitherto directed with judgment, though not with brilliant success. The elevation of de Grasse gave umbrage to many officers in the navy, and involved him in difficulties which ultimately dimmed by a fearful reverse, the laurels won in the earlier part of his naval campaign. The estimate formed of him by most writers then and now is not colored by the respect which success inspires. That of Guérin in his *Histoire Maritime de la France*, is pointed. "Obedience galled him, and as a natural result he brought to command a biting hauteur marque, and a disposition that never stooped to conciliate. If he was not deficient in activity, his mind was certainly destitute of comprehensive grasp, and as he showed but too clearly he was capable of sacrificing a whole plan of operations to a single detail. Brave and good as captain of a ship, the Count de Grasse was an embarrassing commodore, and a still more ill-starred admiral."

The following pages give two cotemporary narratives of his campaign, one by a friendly hand, if not his own, the other representing the party adverse to him on the French navy.

Both describe in detail his actions in the West Indies, his generous exertions and prompt correspondence with Washington's designs against Cornwallis, his brilliant action with Graves off the mouth of the Chesapeake, and then his indecisive affair with Hood, and most disastrous engagement with Rodney, resulting in the loss of so many French vessels and the surrender of his flagship and himself into the hands of the English.¹

After his return to France from England, the king refused him audience, the honors bestowed on Rochambeau were withheld from him, and his conduct was investigated in a council of war held at Lorient. Though he was exonerated and several of his inferior officers censured, he was never again in active service, but lived in retirement till his death, January 14, 1788.²

He was three times married: 1st, in 1764, to Antoinette Rosalie Accaron, daughter of Jean Augustin Accaron, commissary in the navy; 2d, to Catharine Pien, widow of M. de Villeneuve, 3d, to Christine

---

¹ In one of his letters he thus sums up the whole affair: "I have been beaten after an engagement of seven hours, with six ships against fourteen I have surrendered under such circumstances, as that my friends need not blush for me, when they see me again The English fleet has been more successful than the king's and is also under a little better discipline"

² Washington, in a letter to the Count de Rochambeau, who announced the death of their fellow commander at Yorktown, says: "I am sorry to learn that the Count de Grasse, our gallant coadjutor in the capture of Cornwallis, is no more Yet his death is not perhaps so much to be deplored as his latter days were to be pitied It seemed as if an unfortunate and unrelenting destiny pursued him to destroy the enjoyment of all earthly comfort The disastrous battle of the 12th of April, the loss of the favor of his king, and the subsequent connexion in marriage with an unworthy woman, were sufficient to have made him weary of the burden of life Your goodness in endeavoring to sweeten its passage was truly commendable, however it might have been marred by his own impetuosity. But his frailties should now be buried in the grave with him, while his name will be long deservedly dear to this country, on account of his successful cooperation in the former campaign of 1781"

Marie Delphine Lazare de Cibon, a union fruitful to him in unhappiness.

By his first wife he had issue: 1 Alexander François Auguste de Grasse Rouville, Count de Grasse, Marquis de Tilly, who died about 1849. 2. Amélie Rosalie Maxime, who died unmarried. 3. Adelaide, who died at Charleston, S C., August 23, 1799. 4 Maxime de Grasse, knight of Malta, who died in 1773. 5. Melanie Véronique Maxime, who died at Charleston, Sept 19, 1799. 6. Sylvie de Grasse, who married M. Francis de Pau, and died in New York, January 5, 1855, aged 83.

Death removed the Count de Grasse from the scene of life before the storm of revolution swept over his native land, but his surviving children were driven by it into exile and reached the United States. Grateful for the services of the father, the government of the republic made the young count engineer of Georgia and the Carolinas, and bestowed a pension of a thousand dollars a year on the daughters, a fitting return to the family of one who mortgaged his private estates to enable him to carry to Washington the money needed for the army. Two of the daughters soon sank victims to the yellow fever, but the youngest, Madame de Pau, was long a resident of New York She left two sons and five daughters. Louis A. de Pau, one of the former, represents the Count de Grasse in the Society of the Cincinnati. The daughters married leading merchants of New York, and the families of Fox, Livingston, Fowler and Coster, can boast of their descent from the distinguished French commander, whose prompt and generous conduct enabled Washington to carry out his sanguine wishes, and brought to a glorious close the long and desolating war of the Revolution.

Notice biographique sur l'Amiral Comte de Grasse (François Joseph Paul) d'après les documents inédits communiqués par M. le Comte Alexandre Fr. Auguste de Grasse, son fils. Paris, 1840, 8vo. pp. 45. Généalogie de la Maison de Grasse. Paris: Imprimerie de E. Brieze, Rue Sainte Anne 55, 1842, 8vo. 55 pp. Papers, communicated by the kindness of Mrs. Drayton.

A
JOHN JOURNAL
OF THE
CRUISE OF THE FLEET OF HIS MOST
CHRISTIAN MAJESTY,
UNDER THE COMMAND OF
THE COUNT DE GRASSE-TILLY,
IN 1781 AND 1782
BY
THE CHEVALIER DE GOUSSENCOURT

LIST OF THE VESSELS OF THE FLEET.

Names of the Vessels.	Armament.	Captain's Name.
Ville de Paris,	104	Count de Grasse.
Auguste,	80	de Bougainville.
Languedoc,	80	Baron d'Aross.
St. Esprit,	80	de Chabert
Citoyen,	74	Déty
Glorieux,	74	Décars.
Souverain,	74	Glandevese.
Diademe,	74	Montéclerc
Zélé,	74	Préville.
Scipion,	74	Clavel,
Northumberland,	74	Briqueville.
Sceptre,	74	Vaudreuil
Hector,	74	Dalain.
Magnanime,	74	Le Begue.
Bourgogne,	74	Charite
Vaillant,	64	Marigny.
Marseillois,	74	D'Espinouse.
César,	74	Castellane.
Hercule,	74	Turpin.
Pluton,	74	D'Albert Rions.
Sagittaire,	60	Montluc.

FRIGATES:

Medée,	40	La Diligente
Aigrette,	82	

FLUTES.

Minautore,	V.	Union.
Fier, V	F	Dédaigneuse
L'Indiscrete,		Le Sensible.
La Nourrice,		L'Aurore.

et les Vx et fregate de l'Inde

CAMPAIGN IN AMERICA.

The fleet of the Count Destaing having arrived very late from Cadiz, prevented the proposed celerity in fitting out a fleet, which was intended originally to sail under the command of Mr. de la Touche Treville,[1] and of which the Count de Grasse obtained the

---

[1] Louis René Madelène Levassor de La Touche-Tréville vice admiral, was born at Rochefort in 1745, of a family already distinguished in the navy. He entered the service as a midshipman, and had risen to the rank of ensign, when by reforms in the navy, he was dropped He then entered the musketeers and obtained a captaincy in the dragoons, but in 1772, succeeded in recovering a commission in the navy When France declared war against England in 1778, he obtained command of the Rossignole, as lieutenant. In the Hermione, in June 1780, he sustained a long combat with the Isis, for which he obtained a captaincy, and was made Chevalier of St. Louis. He then brought out Lafayette, and erected batteries in Rhode Island. In July, 1781, with La Pérouse, he took an English frigate and corvette off Nova Scotia. In 1782, he brought out to the United States three millions livres in gold, and on the way engaged and so disabled the Hector 64, that she went down a few days after He himself was soon after surprised by Elphinstone, and his vessel running on a shoal, he was forced to strike, and was carried to England where he remained till the peace On his return to France he occupied several posts, but on the breaking out of the revolution, though a deputy of the noblesse, joined the commons. As rear-admiral, he sailed to Naples in 1792, but was the next year deprived of his rank and sent to La Force as a noble Restored to the navy in 1799, he baffled Nelson at Boulogne in 1801, and in the same year reduced Port-au-Prince in St Domingo. He died on board the Bucentaire Aug 19, 1804, while commandant at Toulon

command by his intrigues at court.¹ The vessels that had made the campaign in America under the Count de Guichen,² where they had sustained three combats with the celebrated Rodney,³ had

[1] Chas et Lebrun, in their Histoire de la Revolution de l'Amérique septentrionale, dedicated to Napoleon, also assert that de Grasse obtained the command by intrigue The second journal in this volume gives the opposite account, and states that he took the command reluctantly

[2] Luc Urbain de Bouexie, Count de Guichen, born in Brittany in 1712, midshipman in 1730, passed through all grades up to a captaincy in 1756. In the Ville de Paris he was as commodore at the battle of Ouessant in July 1778, and the next year as lieutenant-general, commanded one of the three great divisions of the fleet. He twice successfully engaged Rodney in April and May 1780, in the West Indies In December of next year, he allowed Kempenfeld to sweep off part of his convoy containing reinforcements for the West Indies, thus greatly embarrassing the Count de Grasse. He commanded the Brest fleet in 1782, and died in 1790.

[3] George Bridges, Lord Rodney, K B , (son of Henry Rodney of Walton upon Thames, the commander of the yacht in which George II and the Duke of Chandos used to visit Hanover,) had the king and that nobleman for his sponsors in baptism, and by their advice was educated for the navy He was born in December 1718, and entering the navy at an early age, became in 1742 lieutenant of the Namur, under admiral Matthews, and was promoted the same year to the Plymouth, 60, as captain, and protected the Lisbon fleet of merchantmen in a way to merit high applause After commanding successively the Sheerness, and the Ludlow Castle, 44, with the latter of which he took the great St Maloes privateer, he next captured two French privateers off the Irish coast in October 1746, being at the time in command of the Eagle, 60 The next year he served in commodore Fox's squadron, which captured a part of the convoy under the escort of M Bois de la Mothe, Rodney taking six of the prizes He next served in admiral Hawke's squadron in the engagement with M. de Letendeur In March, 1749, he was appointed to the Rainbow, and made Governor of Newfoundland He was subsequently in command of the Kent, 74, and Prince George, 90 In 1757, he sailed in the Dublin, under Hawke and Boscawen, first to the French coast, then

joined vice admiral D'Estaing at Cadiz, and reached Brest only on the second of January. Our whole fleet was in the roads on the first of March, and I leave all to judge, in what state it must have been,

---

to Louisburg. In June, 1759, he became rear admiral of the blue, and sailed with a squadron to bombard Havre, and remained off that coast the next year checking the French naval efforts.

In October, 1761, he was sent to the West Indies, and with general Monckton, reduced Martinique, Granada, St. Lucia, and St. Vincent, and by his activity and vigilance, upheld the English power. He was made a baronet, January 21, 1764, governor of Greenwich Hospital in 1765, vice admiral of the white and red in 1770, and rear admiral of Great Britain in 1771.

He was several times in parliament, but the last time secured his election by such liberal use of money as to become a bankrupt, and an exile in France. He refused, however, all offers of preferment in the French service, and in 1778, he was enabled, by the kindness of the Duke de Biron, who furnished him a thousand guineas, to return to England. The next year he was appointed in command of the Leeward Islands. Sailing with a fleet on the 8th of January, 1780, he captured a large Spanish squadron, and on the 16th of the same month, engaged the Spanish squadron under Don Juan de Langara, whom he entirely defeated, taking the admiral's flagship, the Phenix, and four others. Having thus neutralized the efforts of the French and Spaniards against Gibraltar, he landed reinforcements and supplies for the garrison of that post. Sailing then to the West Indies, he engaged de Guichen's fleet on the 13th of April, but without any decisive result; after proceeding to New York to assist Admiral Arbuthnot, he returned to the West Indies in December, and made an ineffectual attempt to recover the island of St. Vincent.

On receiving tidings of the commencement of hostilities with Holland, he seized St. Eustatia, confiscating all the property found there, a step which increased his unpopularity. His engagements with de Grasse given in the text, closed his naval career. He had been already superseded, but as he returned in triumph, was created Baron Rodney, of Rodney Stoke, Somerset, with a pension of £2 000 per annum. He died at London, May 24, 1792. He married 1. Lady Jane Compton, sister of the Earl of Northampton, and 2, Henrietta Splecum, and had issue by both.

since the greater part of the Cadiz fleet formed a part of ours, and I can say in truth that we sailed unsupplied with most of the articles absolutely necessary for a long voyage and manned moreover with wretched crews. We were ready to sail, but the sailors being unpaid were screaming like eagles, when Mr de Castrie, minister of the navy, ex-general officer of cavalry, arrived and found means to satisfy them, after knocking at a hundred doors, the treasury being exhausted. He so urged the departure of the fleet that he at last got it under way.

It is an extraordinary thing that this minister has succeeded in winning from the navy a friendship and esteem which that body refuses even to its own members.

1781
March
Departure

The King's fleet, commanded by Lieutenant-General Count de Grasse-Tilly, set sail on Thursday, March 22, 1781, with a convoy of 250 ships, valued at thirty millions (of livres). The shore was lined by crowds of people enjoying the pleasing spectacle of so large a number of vessels, and M. de Castrie[1] and his suite had proceeded to the Port

---

[1] Charles Eugene Gabriel de la Croix, Marshal de Castries, born Feb 25, 1727, the minister here alluded to, had been in the most important campaigns of his time. His first service was as an infantry officer at Dettingen. At the siege of Maestricht in 1748, he was a brigadier. We then find him commissary-general of cavalry and maréchal-de-camp, commanding in Corsica in 1756. He was wounded at Rosbach, fought at Lutzelberg, and took St Goar. Having been created lieutenant-general, he was in 1759 at the battle of Minden, and at Warburg. He took Rhinberg and Wesel, and at Clostercamp defeated the Duke of Brunswick, who, strangely enough, when de Castries died an exile, erected a monument to his memory. He

Rie (an elevated fort commanding the roadstead), whence he contemplated with pleasure, the sea covered with an immense forest, an interesting object for a minister of the navy, and curious to the chief of the *gendarmerie*. He was saluted by the fort on his arrival, and soon after by the *Ville de Paris*, which was opposite to him. They enabled him to form an opinion on naval collisions, for he witnessed two cases, and they must have augured well in his mind as to the experience of the officers employed in the fleet. By evening we were out of sight of the coast and its fortunate inhabitants, whose happy lot was surely envied, for a Frenchman never leaves his native land without grief, or at least without a regret, which cannot be defined

The slow sailing of the ships in the convoy long retarded us by the little headway they made, for all the favorable winds; still we doubled Cape Finisterre on Sunday, the 25th,[2] on which day we fell in with a Swedish snow. In the evening, a cutter started for Brest to announce our getting out, and it took letters for our home. Many of us did not write, so tortured

---

was dangerously wounded at Amoeneburg, Sept 22, 1762 Other offices were entrusted to him from his activity and energy, and he was successively commander in chief of gendarmerie, governor-general of Flanders and Hainaut, and in 1780, as stated in the text, minister of the navy. In 1785 he was created marshal of France Faithful to the dynasty which he had served so gallantly, he retired into exile at the revolution, and died at Wolfenbuttel, January 11, 1801

[2] The next account says 27th

were they by sea sickness, a disease which meets no pity, though it richly deserves it.

The winds being constantly favorable, on Thursday the 29th, the India division, under the Bailly de Suffren,[1] the *Héron, Annibal, Sphynx, Vengeur*, and *Artésien*, with forty merchantmen, left us. We were then opposite Lisbon, about one hundred and fifty leagues off. The wind fell and it was only the next morning that we lost sight of them. At this point, a part of the fleet took vessels in tow, and when we reached the isles, every one of us had a train.

April. On the 2nd of April, we were off Madeira, thirty leagues distant. At five next morning, order for forward chase; evening, order to form in

---

[1] Pierre André de Suffren de St. Tropez was born at St. Cannat in Provence, July 13, 1726, and was the third son of the Marquis de St. Tropez. He entered the navy in 1743 during the war, and was almost immediately in action. He was in the Trident, in the Duke d'Anville's squadron, sent against Cape Breton, and his vessel was one of the few that escaped the disasters that befell the expedition. In the engagement with Admiral Hawkes off Bellisle, Oct. 25, 1747, he fought as ensign on the *Monarque* till she struck. After the peace of Aix-la-Chapelle, he went to Malta and entering the order of St. John of Jerusalem, made his regular caravans; but on the breaking out of war again, the Chevalier de Suffren embarked on the *Dauphin Royal*, in the fleet of Count Dubois de la Mothe, for Canada. He next served in the Mediterranean fleet under the Marquis de la Galissonière as Lieutenant of the Orphée, and took part in Byng's defeat, but in 1759 was taken on the port of Lagos by the English. He became captain of a frigate in 1767, captain of a ship of the line in 1772, having in the interval attained the grade of commander in his order. When France took part in our revolutionary struggle, the commander de Suffren, as captain of the *Fantasque*, served in d'Estaing's fleet, and was sent from Boston to take five English frigates at Newport. He then took part in the capture of Grenada, in the engagement with

line of battle, which was executed only next morning, so much good will was there in the fleet and convoy, which had the air of amusing itself to prevent the manœuvre; this is a pretty fair specimen of the military subordination in our ships generally, and the royal navy especially.

Here for the first time, I perceived the effect which the sea has on dispositions. The lieutenant of the store ships flew into a passion with a poor clerk, who had perhaps done his duty too conscientiously, and gave him slaps, blows, etc., a very ordinary cere-

---

Byron, and blockaded Savannah with a squadron prior to the assault In the *Zelé*, in 1780, he formed part of the French-Spanish fleet under Don Luis de Cordova, and perceiving the advantage of coppering ships, urged it on government. In 1780, he was sent with a squadron to protect the Cape of Good Hope against the English, and set out as stated in the text with the Count de Grasse, bearing as a marine the future king of Sweden, Bernadotte. On the 16th of April, he engaged Commodore Johnston in La Praya bay. After protecting the cape he joined the fleet of Count d'Orves, and on his death took the command. He engaged Admiral Hughes off Sadras Feb 17, 1782, again off Provedien, April 12, and off Negapatam, July 6. Received with high honor by Hyder Ali, Suffren, now Bailli, besieged and took Trinquemale, beating off the English fleet. Holland struck a medal in his honor and ordered Houdon to execute his bust.

In June, 1783 he forced Hughes to raise the blockade of Cuddalore, and again engaged his fleet. The news of the peace arrested his further proceedings.

On his return to France he was received with great honors, his own Provence struck a medal to commemorate his service; and the king created him vice-admiral of France. He died at Paris, December 8 1788, when on the point of proceeding to Brest to take command of a fleet.

Hennequin, *Essai Historique sur la vie et les campagnes du Bailli du Suffren*, Paris, 1824, 8° Compare Andrews. *History of the War*, &c iv. 320–357

mony in the king's ships, where a clerk is rated about as a dog.

On the 4th, we found ourselves under the trade winds, so called, because they always blow in the same direction, are very gentle, and consequently render the sea beautiful.

On the 5th, the *Sagittaire* steered for Boston, taking thirty vessels as a convoy.[1]

The next day we were becalmed and the general made all form in line. On the return of our boat, we learned from an officer who came from the *Ville de Paris*, that the English were at sea with a fleet of 28 vessels, and a convoy of 200, going to Gibraltar or America, Mr. de Grasse proposing to give them a sound thrashing if he met them. So he promised us, but he did not keep his word.

On the 9th, the calm having ceased, we held on our way, and nothing eventful occurred till the 12th, when we witnessed the swamping of a boat, which showed that form of death in all its horrors.

It is usual for vessels sailing as a fleet, to do the butchering with their neighbors; ours had been killing, and the captain ordered the boat to be lowered to go and get meat; we were then running four knots

---

[1] These vessels carried six hundred and sixty recruits for Rochambeau's army, and reached Boston in June, four hundred only being fit for duty. The Abbé Robin, author of a volume of travels, came as chaplain with this body. The *Sagittaire* bore a letter from de Grasse to Rochambeau, dated at sea, March 29, proposing joint action. An extract will be found in Sparks's *Washington*, viii, 76.

an hour, that is to say, we were making about four miles an hour; we did not lie to to effect this operation, although the sea was running high; the boat was let down, but the sailors forgot to make it fast behind, which caused their ruin; for as the vessel held on, the swell taking the boat, drove it against the ship and soon stove it in; the water rushing in would have swamped it at once, had it not been made fast; the next swell dashed the boat against the ship and it went to pieces, the little crew did all they could to save the boat, but in vain; it soon went down, and I saw the poor fellows, five in all, go down with the fragments, I saw the master come up, then three of the sailors; the first got on board, the other three, while he was getting up, had disappeared in spite of the ropes thrown out to them, and all that it was humanly possible to do to save them, then he sprang into the water, dived, and brought up by the hair two men whom he rescued from the jaws of death, he has them hoisted up, and in a manner devoting himself to certain death, in spite of the cries of the crew, he dove again and rescued his third comrade from death, then he swam around the vessel, looking for the last of his party whose head he saw crushed between the fragments of the boat and the vessel. Then he got on board, met the captain, asked pardon for losing the boat and a man, and having obtained forgiveness, asked the command of another boat, and having received it, went next day for his meat. What an example of firmness did not this man give! Surely, among the Romans he would have obtained the civic crown.

Our voyage continuing favorable, there came up with evening an extraordinary courier of the good old Tropic, to announce to the staff and all the crew, that we would next morning enter the torrid zone, a vast country belonging to his master: that he would come in person, attended by a numerous staff of officers and his high priest, to pay a visit to the captain and those whom he had long known, and to proclaim to the others that no one could sail in the burning region without being first purified and aspersed with the bitter wave, enjoining on each one to examine himself. He made protestations of sincere fridndship on behalf of his master, to his old acquaintances Then with a terrible and very disagreeable noise he returned to the mast head.

Baptism On the 13th, at six o'clock in the morning, we heard an extraordinary symphony in the mastheads and rigging; it was old Tropic's couriers. One put himself on guard at the cabin door to await the captain's waking and ask him his hour; he replied that he would be pleased to see his sable majesty at ten. In consequence, at half-past nine down from the mizzen mast head came twenty sailor boys all naked and all black; they began the march, and announced at the top of their lungs the coming of the hideous sovereign, holding a cup of water in his hand;

then down from the foretop came the high priest, robed in white, with white beard and wig, preceded by twelve men bearing books and torches to swear people in; all these ranged themselves on the right. Soon after a superb car appeared in the main top, formed of shells of sea monsters, drawn by four sharks. This descended to the sound of a rude f—g, mingled with the sound of the extraordinary instruments that had been heard from daybreak. It was preceded by twelve old fellows, younger brothers of the sable monarch, all dressed in red, trimmed with various colors. They ranged themselves on the right while their elder brother got out of his chariot and went to pay his compliments to the captain. On his return, he again entered his chariot, and ordered his high priest to begin the ceremonies. He accordingly took a seat in front of a table, while two of his people took their seats on stools, beside a tub full of water over which was a plank. An ensign was called and put on the board near the table, and surrounded by the suite of the head chaplain, who asked him his age, how many voyages, by what straits, and on what sea he had sailed; of how many male children he was father, with the circumstantial details of all, whether he had had any connexion with a sailor's wife or daughter; after this they threw water on his head; meanwhile the plank was slipped away and my gentleman found himself with his back in the water, caught so that he could not stir. Then a glass of water was poured on his head, his forehead daubed black, and a plate presented in which he must put a silver piece, after which he was taken out. Another succeeds him, and so it goes through the staff and gentlemen on board, passengers as well as others. After this there falls a heavy rain from the topmasts, wetting everything; the buckets along the vessel are constantly filled and poured over some one's back. This is kept up some six hours, and during this last ceremony the sable sovereign, the high priest, and their suite, are at the caboose (place where victuals are given out), getting drunk with the money that they have received; this debauch lasts usually three or four days.

Good wind and sea high. On the 18th, the admiral despatched the cutter *Pandour* to Martinique to announce to Mr. du Bouillé,[1] governor of the Windward isles, the arrival of the fleet, and the rich convoy, which was expected with the greatest impatience, as our isles were destitute of many things, and the storehouses empty.

---

[1] Francis Claude Amour, Marquis de Bouillé, a native of Auvergne, served first in the dragoons and rose to the rank of marechal de camp He was made governor-general of the Windward isles, where he greatly distinguished himself. On his return he was made lieutenant-general and proposed for the command of a projected invasion of India At the commencement of the French revolution he reduced an insurrection at Nancy, and endeavored to effect a compromise, but took flight when the king was arrested He endeavored to induce the king of Sweden to aid Louis XVI and on the assassination of the former, retired to London, where he died Nov 14, 1800, aged 62 He wrote memoirs on the French revolution, published in English, at London, in 1797, and in the original at Paris in 1801

The 19th, we took and eat a little fish called the pilot fish, about ten or twelve inches long, with firm white flesh. It takes its name from serving as a guide to the shark, to the back of which it fastens itself when it finds an opportunity, and lives by the oil that exudes from the pores of that frightful animal. The sucker is another little fish which also lives on the oil of the shark, but it is difficult to separate it, and I saw one that they could not get off, and so the crew eat it with the shark to which it adhered. This fish is very delicate. I also saw goldfish and dolphin, which is absolutely the most beautiful kind of fish possible, it is about thirty inches long, gold, azure, mingling with a ground of green, which forms a most agreeable variety. Its flesh greatly resembles mackerel. When this fish is out of water it becomes green, spotted with gold, and when dead it is white. The male dolphin preserves its colors longer when taken; it is also longer and thicker than the female. This fish is very voracious, and so is the bonite, which is two to three feet long, and always in pursuit of the flying fish. Its flesh is very dry, even more so than the goldfish, not being as good as the latter, and living further from the shore.

On the 22d, we were separated from the rest of the fleet. How sad a spectacle is that of a solitary vessel! What a vast desert does not the solitude of the sea then present! To see only the sky and the waves, two or three hundred leagues from land! What a secret pain does not a man then experience, who, accustomed to live with his fellowmen, lives but with the fish. The next day I again beheld the fleet and the convoy, to my great satisfaction; for I should have died had nothing diverted me from the gloomy reflections in which I was plunged. We took a merchant vessel in tow, and the whole fleet was soon crowding sail.

On the 24th, I had the pleasure of seeing birds. Ah, what joy I felt. This assured us that we were not over one hundred and fifty leagues from land, and this pleasure was a lively one for all; I also saw flying fish for the first time. This little animal seven or eight inches long, white as a swan, rises some fifteen or twenty feet from the sea, when it is pursued by the bonites or goldfish, and skims through the air a distance of perhaps two hundred fathoms, then it plunges again into the sea to moisten its wings, and is often caught by its enemies which swim as fast as it flies. They are generally three or four hundred together. This fish is really the most delicate of all meats. They can be taken only when they fall on board, and this happens quite frequently in small vessels. I also saw a kind of vegetation called galères, which is very singular; it bears no resemblance to Flemish caps, but burns also; the galère is six to eight inches long, with a kind of pivot in the middle which it raises at will, and on which are two fan looking wings that act as sails. When it hoists its mast it is a sure sign of wind. It is of a violet color with a little red.

As they sail pretty fast it was a pastime for us in American seas, to examine whether they were mast up, for in those parts calms abound.

On the 27th, we took a shark, twenty feet long, three feet and a half in diameter, the head twenty inches long, the mouth armed with seven ranges of teeth, three of which are inflexible. I have seen these animals take in the head, arms, and thighs of a man thrown overboard during or after a fight. This fish is full of an oil of very offensive odor, but this does not prevent the sailors from eating it. In the stomach of this one they found a shoe, a fish half digested, and some cards.

On Saturday, the 28th, at 8 A. M., our watch cried "land ahead!" It was in fact the Morne[1] du Vauclin, a mountain on the west side of Martinique, from which we were twelve or fifteen leagues off. Signal to clear for action: at noon we saw the land quite distinctly. The *Northumberland's* boat went ashore to bring off news from the island, the *Pandour* not having come up, the admiral learned that the English had been blockading our ports for a month. Signal to the fleet to prepare for action next day, and orders to beat all night; orders to the convoy to close in, and to its escort to keep good watch. We plied to windward all night and were signaled from St. Lucia.

---

[1] The word morne, which frequently occurs in these journals, is a term for mountain, used in the French West Indies. As some French islands passed into the hands of the English, they still retained the word

Action of Martinique.

Sunday, 29th, at 6 A. M. Signal for mass on all the ships of the fleet; at half-past six, signal for crews to breakfast; at seven to prepare for action, and for the fleet to hug the shore of Martinique, consequently to keep before the wind; at eight, the frigate in the van signalled twenty-three sail, and she soon distinguished eighteen English ships of the line, and five frigates or corvettes; at nine the captain ordered us to leave our breakfast and take our posts, an order already given to the crew, for they were all at the guns. We were in battle in the natural order, and the English fleet, very well formed, came down on us under heavy sail, with the confidence inspired by certainty of success, supposing us only ten or twelve vessels. At half-past nine, they were athwart the Diamond, a rock at the extremity of Martinique, towards St. Lucia, when the Count de Grasse hoisted his flag, and at once the *Languedoc* fired on the enemy, but the balls did not reach, and when they came up, the English let themselves bear away, having made us out to be twenty ships of the line, and losing the hope of carrying off any vessels of our convoy, they tacked and came on the larboard tack like us. Signal to the French fleet to tack in succession. This tended to bring us nearer to the enemy, and succeeded to a certain point, but it was very easy to bring them more under our fire, as we were to the windward of them, and what did our admiral risk with his twenty vessels? Mr. D'Albert St. Hippolyte,¹ came out of Fort Royal with four vessels, the *Victoire*, 74, the *Solitaire*, 64, commanded by Mr. de Cicé, the *Reflechi*, 64, de Marigny, the *Cato*, 64, de Framont, so as to cover the entrance of the convoy, which did not need it, and which took no part in the action. At noon the wind fell and we were, so to say, becalmed; four English vessels ran afoul of each other, and were separated from their fleet; it has been decided by naval officers of some experience, that they ought to have been cut off and taken, the *Souverain* marked the manœuvre. Mr. de Grasse paid no attention to it, and commodore Bougainville,² would not

---

¹ The Chevalier d'Albert St Hippolyte, became a commodore, January 12, 1782, and Champion de Cicé attained the same rank, August 20, 1784. De Waroquier, *Etat Général de la France*. The latter a native of Rennes, in Brittany, was a brother of Mgr de Cicé, Bishop of Auxerre, and of Mgr de Cicé, Archbishop of Bordeaux, keeper of the seals to Louis XVI. *Biographie Bretonne*. The Viscount de Marigny, who fell so nobly on his vessel the *Cesar*, after defending her to the last in the fatal battle of April 12, 1782, was a brother of the more famous Charles de Bernard, Viscount de Marigny, who brought Franklin over in the Belle Poule in 1778.

² Louis Antoine, Count de Bougainville, the son of a notary, was born at Paris, November 11, 1729. To please his family he studied law and was admitted to the bar, but his mathematical taste led him to the army. After publishing a work on the Integral Calculus in 1752, he served in the army as aid major and aid de camp. While temporary secretary of legation at London in 1754, his literary ambition was gratified by being made a member of the Royal Society. In 1756, he came to Canada as aid de camp to Montcalm, with the brevet grade of captain of dragoons. Here his career was a most brilliant one, and at Lake George, at Abercrombie's defeat, and in most of the actions of the war, he displayed courage, activity, and military skill. In 1758, he repaired to France to obtain reinforcements, and presented to the court four memorials on the military de-

take the responsibility on him; although it would have been much more honorable than to pass to the windward of several vessels that were engaged with the enemy to the leeward. Our fleet then entered Fort Royal, Martinique, and presented a most agreeable spectacle; the land on one side, the English on the other, and our fleet, formed four very interesting groups. All efforts to bring Admiral Hood[1] to close

---

fence of Canada, which show no ordinary talent. The cross of St. Louis rewarded his past exertions, but his eloquence was unavailing. He returned to fight the desperate fight on the St. Lawrence, and was ever in the van. Even after the fall of Quebec, he was at Isle aux Noix disputing every inch with Amherst. When Vaudreuil capitulated, he returned to France and then served with distinction in Germany. Having taken a fancy for naval affairs, he obtained a captaincy in the navy, and attempted to form a settlement at the Falkland Isles, but was appointed by government to surrender the islands to Spain, after which he made his celebrated voyage around the world, making many discoveries in the Pacific. He returned to St. Malo in 1769, and published an account of his voyage in 1771. The war with England called him into active service. He commanded the *Guerrier*, 74, at Savannah in 1778-9, and was made commodore; in de Grasse's fleet he commanded the *Auguste*, 80. Strangely enough his next promotion was to be marechal-de-camp in the army in 1780. In 1790, he endeavored in vain to restore order in the fleet of d'Albert de Rions. He was one of the vice-admirals of 1792. In 1796, he was made a member of the Institute in the section of geography, and became under Napoleon, senator and count of the empire. He died August 31, 1811. Besides the works already mentioned, he wrote an account of the Indians of North America. *Biographie Universelle.* O'Callaghan, *New York Colonial Documents*, x. 1124. Dussieux, *Le Canada Sous la Domination Française.*

[1] Samuel, Viscount Hood of Whitley, was born in 1724, at Butley, Somersetshire; entered the navy at the age of sixteen. In 1757, he was captain of the *Antelope*, 50, and captured a French frigate. Post captain in 1759, he took part in the expedition against Quebec, capturing the Bellona. In 1768-9, he was at Boston commander-in-chief

action failed, our van was the only division of our fleet, that could at all approach him. The action lasted from half-past nine till three; we lost only one officer killed, one dangerously wounded, and one hundred and fifty men killed or wounded. Hood manœuvered in vain to enter St. Lucia, but was prevented by our fleet, which might and should have done him much injury.[1] Admiral Rodney was then busy pillaging St. Eustatia the only Dutch emporium in the Windward Isles. We pursued the English for three days ineffectually, although they had tried false routes, but as they were faster sailors, being all copper-sheathed, and our fleet half and half, our vessels too,

---

of all the men of war in those parts, and involved in the affair of the *Rose* frigate. In 1778, he was made a baronet, and in 1780, rear admiral of the blue. For his part in the victory of de Grasse, he was made Baron Hood of Catherington, in the peerage of Ireland, and promoted to the chief command of the flee. His great achievement was however the destruction of the French arsenal and fleet at Toulon, in 1793, and his expulsion of the French from Corsica in 1794, for which he was made viscount and grand cross of the order of the Bath. He was also appointed governor of Greenwich Hospital which office he held till his death at Bath, June 27, 1816, at the age of 92.

[1] The other journal gives a different account, and ascribes the escape of Hood to the neglect of the French van to come into action. It mentions the *Russel*, *Centaur*, *Torbay*, and *Intrepid*, as having suffered most in the English line, and Hood's letter to Rodney admits the sinking condition of the *Russel*. His loss he gives as 36 killed and 161 wounded, principally on the *Centaur*, *Russel*, *Shrewsbury*, and *Gibraltar*, which were very much damaged, and the *Centaur* losing her captain and first lieutenant. Andrews' *History of the War*, iv, 131. Almon's *Rem.*, xii, 178. *History of the Civil War in America*, iii, 217. According to a report cited by the latter writer, Hood was opposed to cruising off Fort Royal bay, preferring a cruize off Point Salines.

being much embarrassed with merchandise, it is not surprising that we did not overtake them; but it is astonishing that Mr. de Grasse should have committed the fault of letting four vessels escape that he might have taken; this led to a dispute at St. Pierre, between Commodore Bougainville and several navy officers: the origin of an ill feeling that afterwards prevailed in the fleet.

The action had been over about an hour, and we were at table, when a noise like that of an eight pounder was heard in the second battery We went down and found a gunner killed and three wounded; it was a priming horn that had exploded and killed the careless fellow who was examining it, seated on a large tub full of water, in which they plunge the linstocks, and three of his comrades who were talking ten paces off, were severely wounded. (The priming horn is a cow's horn, in which the priming of the cannon is put and which is used to press the powder into the touch-hole.)

May   The chase of the English having made us fall to leeward, it cost us some pains to regain the island of Martinique, and we anchored off the fort only on the sixth of May in the afternoon, with orders to land our sick at once. The last vessel had scarcely anchored when the admiral signaled to prepare to make sail. In fact on the eighth, at four P. M., we were under sail making for the channel of St. Lucia. Mr. de Bouillé had embarked in the morning on vessels called *Domaines*, which belong to the king, cost him extravagantly, and never fulfil their mission, being commanded by beggars, who have absolutely no object but to make a fortune, and who care little for the interests of the state. They had on board a part of the regiments of Champagne, Auxerrois, Viennois, Dillon, and Martinique, which landed by night at St Lucia, and I have been told by officers who were present, that had the English kept good watch, a landing would have been impracticable. Meanwhile we cruized in the channel and were fortunate enough to pass it. Then it was that the *Pluton* and the *Experiment*, a vessel of 50, which had joined us at Fort Royal, were detached to blockade and if possible take Tobago.[1]

On the 11th, the *Saint Esprit* was run into by the *Sceptre*, and without the admiral's order, put back to Martinique to repair her bowsprit, which was unserviceable: the *Sceptre* received only a slight damage.

On the 13th, at 3, we anchored in the old roadstead of St. Lucia, in Gros Islet bay, where a battery annoyed us considerably. There were five or six others that kept up a brisk fire, but not being so well posted, and the calibre being smaller, they were ineffectual, in fact only saluted us, but seven or eight of our vessels being too near Gros Islet, were obliged to weigh anchor and draw in towards the anchorage of

---

[1] The second journal says that d'Albert de Rions's squadron was one ship of the line, and two 50 gunships, with transports carrying land troops under M de Blanchelande

the *Ville de Paris*, after asking and being refused leave to return the fire, although there were five or six men wounded and three killed.[1]

On the 16th, in the morning, our long boats and barges went ashore to bring off the troops there and the prisoners they had taken amounting to one hundred and fifty men and two officers. Mr. de Bouillé saw clearly that the Morne Fortuné required a regular siege which could not be undertaken except by an army of twenty thousand men and its train.[2] The enemy made no greater opposition to our reembarkation than they had to the landing of our troops, and we set sail at six A. M.

The brilliant manœuvres that they made us perform in the channel kept us till the 18th, when we again anchored off Fort Royal.

On the 25th we set sail once more, after taking in water, and we again ran up the channel of St Lucia. Our wretched sailors so alarmed an English frigate that she was lost on the coast of St. Lucia.[3]

On the 29th, at daybreak, we discovered Tobago on one side, and on the other, seven English vessels and

---

[1] The English battery that drove them off was on Pigeon Island. Breen's *St Lucia*, 69

[2] The second journal better explains this affair, de Bouillé had an idea of fortifying Gros Islet as a check on the English work at Morne Fortuné, but found on examination that there was not time enough to throw up sufficient works. He seems to have had no idea of attacking the English fort

[3] This was the Thetis, 74, which struck while trying to enter Carenage bay. Breen's *St Lucia*, 70

five frigates,[1] coming to the relief of that isle, and which would have taken the *Pluton* and *Experiment* had we not arrived. We gave them chase but to no purpose, for they were three leagues to our windward. In the evening the *Aigrette* asked leave to give chase, and at nine she took a brig of ten guns.

On the 31st, being under Tobago, we made several sail. Our chasers to the number of three, hoisted the English flag, as did several vessels of the fleet, and the sail we had discovered came and threw themselves into our hands. A slaver which we did not see, and which had at least two hundred and fifty negroes on board, did the same, and in the evening, as well as the next day, we took several more small vessels.

June Capture of Tobago

On the 2d of June, about 4, P. M, the fleet all anchored off Tobago, except the *St. Esprit* and *Glorieux*, which remained cruising along the shore of the island. It had surrendered the previous evening to Mr. de Bouillé, who had landed with eight hundred men three days before. The apparition of our fleet, the slight relief they could expect, and the reputation of the commander on shore, had induced them to lay down their arms.[2] Notwithstanding the reputation for humanity, which Mr. de

---

[1] This was Drake, who, according to Gordon, had six sail of the line, some frigates, a regiment, and two additional companies, for the relief of the island.

[2] These operations are detailed in the second journal and in the extract from the *Journal de France*

Bouillé had most deservedly acquired, a number of the inhabitants had fled to the hills where they had taken their cattle, a part of which was found slaughtered. We made them return to their houses without doing them any harm, only that a few of Dillon's soldiers, and the crews of the *Pluto* and *Experiment* commanded by Mr. de Martelly,[1] pillaged a little. The last named officer found he had on board all the bells of the houses, which they had taken on their arrival, amounting to twenty-nine. The capture of Tobago cost us only three men. We took there ten officers and three hundred and sixty men, and left a garrison of eighteen hundred men, arms and money.

Tobago is twenty leagues in circumference. It has only 18,000 negroes. The air is very unhealthy, the soil very dry, covered with swarms of ants, which blight the sugar cane, so that they raise only cotton. Its port is small, and its roadsteads many, and as secure probably as the best ports in the West Indies.

On the afternoon of the third, we set sail again, in consequence of the signals made by the *Glorieux* and *St. Esprit*, which had remained cruising, and had discovered the enemy's fleet. It was in fact, the celebrated Rodney coming to the relief of Tobago, but

---

[1] The second journal speaks of this squadron as being commanded by the Chevalier d'Albert de Riom. This naval officer was a native of Dauphiny. He was subsequently a commodore and commanded the fleet at Cherbourg in 1786 when Louis XVI visited it, and embarked on his vessel the Patriot. In 1790 he commanded at Brest. He served under Condé against the Republicans in 1792, and died in 1810.

learning that it was taken, he would not hazard an action that could result only in mutual slaughter, the fleets being of equal force. Monsieur de Grasse, on the contrary, sought to engage the English; but being to leeward, he could not overtake them.

On the 6th we entirely lost sight of them, and would have entertained fears for the *Hector* had it not left us five or six days before for Granada, the only port where she could put in, being in a most wretched plight since she ran foul of the *Cæsar*; the *Medée*, in spite of her injuries, succeeded in getting safe into the port, which is small but very secure; it might even be enlarged to twice the size with a little outlay.

Our chase of the English having made us fall considerably to leeward, on the morning of the 8th, our admiral asked the bearings of several vessels, and the whole fleet watched carefully for the signals; for so little attention had been paid to the route we had made, that probably no one except Mr de Chabert,[1] knew where he was. Fortunately, however, at noon

---

[1] John Bernard, Marquis de Chabert, was born at Toulon in 1723 He entered the navy as ensign in 1758, and by his ability, especially as a scientific man and gallant officer, rose to be vice-admiral and lieutenant-general in the navy He died December 2, 1805, aged 62 As a hydrographer, he rendered essential service to the French marine He was sent in 1750 by the king to rectify the maps of the coasts of Acadia, Cape Breton, and Newfoundland, and to fix the principal points by astronomical observations. On his return he published an account of his voyage at Paris in 1753 in 4 vols The allusion to him in the text shows that he was considered as the scientific man in the service

the direction of all was good; for we discovered Granada on one side and our new conquest on the other, about thirty leagues apart. We anchored off Granada the tenth.

This island is very beautiful and good; it produces sugar in abundance and certainly the best rum in the West Indies. It is very well defended, the French having added many works to what the English had already when Vice-admiral Count Destain captured it. The population is considerable, since the negroes amount to 64,000. Mr. de Bouillé, who continued with us, as well as the troops in the expedition, distributed them among the different islands, and put every thing in the best possible order, and best state of defence.

On the 13th, the fleet again set sail and lay to before St. Vincent, waiting for the general of the troops, who had gone there the day before. Mean while several periaguas full of Caribs boarded us, and offered us tobacco, which in my opinion is good for nothing and affects the head greatly. The Caribs are copper colored, large, strong, and vigorous; they have the forehead flatter than other negroes. There are none except on this island, and three families in Dominica They never marry out of their tribe, and punish severely any of their women who go with the blacks, or even with the whites.

There grows in this isle, and that of St Lucia, a

tree called Manchenillier,[1] the wood of which when worked, is certainly the handsomest in the West Indies, but which is also one of the most dangerous productions of the country, for it constantly distils a sap which burns more violently than the best vitriol. Those who are so unlucky as to sleep under it, generally lose their eye sight. We saw its sad effects on several of our soldiers, and some even who passed the night under large Manchenilher, which were losing their sap, awaked paralized in the limb on which a drop had fallen. This tree is cut down by fire, and is not worked till thirty years after it is felled; for there are many examples of workmen very dangerously affected on putting the axe to it after twenty years.

I had forgotten, when speaking of St. Lucia, to mention the enormous length and bulk of the rattle snakes, of which that island is full. They are generally twenty or thirty feet long, and large in proportion, and their sting is mortal. They are found also in the other isles, for at Fort Royal in Martinique, I saw one at an apothecary's full twenty-two feet long. The negroes have a mortal fear of this animal. This country is generally full of all kinds of venomous animals, and when you walk around the house you must take precautions to avoid the reptiles which abound there.

On the 18th of June, the fleet anchored at Fort

---

[1] This tree, the Manchineel, was described by Columbus, and poisonous qualities attributed to it. There is possibly some exaggeration about its effects, but its dangerous character is indisputable. *Brande*

Royal, in Martinique. We there learned that during our cruise, a water-spout (a considerable column of air and water), a common thing enough in the West Indies, had fallen partly on that island, in the channel and on St. Lucia's, where it had devastated one canton. Some planters, and many negroes were drowned; and the most distinguished people of the isle had taken refuge on the store ships, the *Union* and the *Fier*, the water having risen to six or seven feet in the streets of Fort Royal. Our admiral gave an entertainment to Mme. de Bouillé, which was returned by her husband; and to his, were invited the ladies of Martinique and the officers of the two forces. These entertainments were not over brilliant, play occupying most of the dancers. I shall have occasion elsewhere to describe what these balls are, and how people act at them · I shall therefore not speak of these. During our stay the frigates visited the different ports of the island, and those of the neighboring isles, to collect all the vessels bound to Cape François, and those that were to return to Europe.

July The 5th of July, the fleet and its convoy of over two hundred vessels, hoisted sail in fine weather, good wind, and beautiful sea. We went to Grenadina, an island dependant on Granada, in search of the *Hector* and a convoy of fifteen sail. After making the junction, we steered for Cape François, while the English, starting from Barbadoes, which had since the affair of April 29th, been their general post, steered for Jamaica, whence Rodney sailed with his treasure for England. He carried along also the prisoners he had taken from us, there being no longer any exchanges in America, from Count de Guichen's arrival in those parts. We had prisoners on our ships during the whole cruise, and finally landed them at Brest.

On the 13th, being off the coast of Porto Rico, and athwart Dead Chest island,[1] we were surprised by a terrible storm. The fleet and convoy were obliged to lay to for several hours, the lightning striking every moment among us.

On the 14th, Commander de Glandevese was detached with four vessels to cruise around St. Domingo and small isles adjacent to the leeward, and to relieve the *Actionnaire*, 74, which we had been assured was blockaded by two English ships of the line, and two frigates.

On the 15th, about 4, P. M., the vessels in the van signalled sails to the windward of the Cape Pass, and when we had passed La Grange, we recognized the division of the Commodore Marquis de Monteuil.[2] It consisted of the *Palmier*, 74, the *Destin*, 74, commanded

---

[1] One of the Virgin islands

[2] Adhemar, Marquis de Monteil, was born in Languedoc, of a family which was famous in the crusades and of which the last descendant is said to be the Lieutenant-colonel Viguier de Monteil, killed at Roanoke in 1862. The marquis commanded the Palmier, 74, in de Guichen's action with Rodney in 1780, took part in the siege of Pensacola, and contributed materially to de Grasse's defeat as we shall see

by Mr. de Goimpy,[1] the *Triton*, 64, Captain Mr. de Pierrefeu, and a frigate. The *Intrépide*, 74, had remained at the anchorage; it had all its masts on shore, as it had suffered considerably in the storm which this little squadron experienced on its way back from the expedition against Pensacola, a place at the extremity of the Gulf of Mexico, and which would never have fallen into the hands of Spain, had not this division and the French infantry taken part in it. It was at this siege that the English, having made a sortie, took a redoubt, and finding the Spaniards all busily engaged in taking their siesta, drove them out by belaboring them in the belly with the butts of their muskets, and by kicks behind, pretending (and perhaps justly) that they were not worth killing, and made prisoner of only one single man, a French gunner, who escaped from them on the way.[2]

At six the fleet entered the pass of Cape François; the convoy was already at anchor, and as the coast pilots preferred going on merchantmen, we did without; and in consequence three or four vessels could not get in till next day by the sea breeze; for in this island, as in all the Antilles, a periodical wind prevails, called the land breeze and sea breeze, the latter begins

---

[1] The Count du Maitz de Goimpy had commanded this vessel in the action with Rodney in May, 1780, and after the close of the war, was made commodore August 20, 1784.

[2] Farmar's journal of the remarkable defence of Pensacola by Col. Campbell, will be found in the *Historical Magazine*, vol iv, p 166

at 8, A. M., and lasts till 5, P. M., then the land breeze follows in the same way. There are seasons when they change as much as two or three times a day, rendering the passage very dangerous.

At the entrance of the roadstead of the cape is a small fort, thrown up rather for the sake of looks than as a defence. Over against it are the Carpenters rocks over which you must pass. There are two channels, both dangerous; and vestiges of several wrecked vessels may be seen there. The roadstead is very extensive, lying before the royal battery of 60 pieces of ordnance, which would not amount to much, I opine, if the town were attacked. I have seen four hundred vessels anchored in the roadstead, and there was still room for fifty more. The town is behind the royal battery. On the other side is the plain in which you find the towns of Limonade and Marmelade. This plain is beautiful. At the head of the bay is a river, easily ascended in small boats and even in long boats, in which we have transported our sick and wounded to a fine hospital, kept by the Hospitallers of St. John of God. It is the best in the West Indies. It was formerly the country house of the Jesuits, whose residence is now the government house.

The town of Cape François passes for being the most agreeable in the West Indies, and justly. It is the Paris of the isles. All go there to know the fashions. It is, too, the handsomest, and next to Havana the richest. For its size and commerce it may be compared to Lyons. Its streets are always full of negroes, rolling " et boucault de sucre et quart de café." Cap François is regularly built; all the streets are straight; the houses are low, not over two stories, built of beautiful stone, in spite of the earthquakes, which, in fact, are no longer so common there; but, in compensation, Port au Prince, on the other side of the island, is constantly subjected to them.

The town is backed by high mountains, which render its position very hot and unhealthy. Its wide streets are always filled with throngs of people, often disturbed by the equipages. There are many pretty fine places, but few remarkable buildings. The government house is handsome; the church pretty fine; the theatre ugly. There is a convent of nuns that does not look ill. This is, I believe, all worth mentioning.

The French part of St. Domingo is intersected by great roads, which are always filled with conveyances, horses and negroes, the only pedestrians of the place. The luxury is extraordinary, so much so that there are more than fifty planters who spend over six or seven thousand francs on mulatto girls. They have come to the wonderful conclusion that morality is impossible in this climate, where all conspires to destroy it. The soil of St. Domingo is excellent, and it is cited as the best in the West Indies; and it is not so exhausted as on the other islands. It is even pretended that its produce exceeds that of Jamaica, though belonging to the English, who are, beyond a doubt, the best cultivators of this torrid region, and most expert in turning it to account.

Nothing memorable or interesting occurred till the 23d, a sad day by our loss upon it. It is the custom on French vessels in America to give the crew brandy or tafia at one meal, and wine at the two others. The strong liquor is given always at breakfast. At half past seven, the *Intrepide*, of 74 guns, made a signal of distress, and no one could imagine what the matter was; for like her neighbor, the *Hector*, she had many mechanics. All supposed that some trouble had broken out between the crew and the people on board the two vessels, the more especially as one was from Brest, the other from Toulon — there existing between the officers of these departments a hatred that extends to all that come from there. At eight o'clock we learned that the *Intrepide* was on fire. The clerk had gone for tafia (a liquor more spiritous than brandy), and seeing that little came out, he held the light near the tap and the flame at once extended to the barrel. He tried to put it out alone, but failing, called his men, who made fruitless efforts to extinguish the fire. A thick smoke which spread over the vessel disclosed what they wished to hide. When the officers first tried to remedy it, they found the caboose on fire. They cut the cable to run the ship ashore away from the others. This was happily effected. Much powder was thrown over-

Conflagration of the Intrepide

board, and all the rest in the magazine was soaked. The gun carriages were broken so as to point the cannons up. All the boats of the fleet and merchantmen, and all the carpenters were at work there, helping all they could, to save the king's property and individual effects. They were even in great apparent security, each busy with his work, when a voice exclaimed: "*Sauve qui peut!*" Then every one rushed to the boats, and soon after a dense black smoke issued from the vast machine, so dense as to darken the air—the sun disappeared from us—we could only see the flames bursting from the portholes. The cannons grew red, and the roadstead, the town, and the shore, received her whole broadside. A fearful noise succeeded the artillery. It was the stern of the vessel, which was in the clouds, scattered in fragments. All around was filled with them, wounding many and killing some. Thus, at half past eleven, ended the *Intrepide*. The townspeople fled, and the consternation was so great that many would not go home for a long time, imagining that the conflagration must extend to other vessels.

The 25th we learned that the French frigate the *Inconstante*, of 40 guns, had the misfortune to be burnt at sea. She took fire in precisely the same way as the *Intrepide*, and blew up two leagues off the coast of St Domingo. A midshipman, two auxiliary officers, and seventy-seven men escaped on loose masts and spars; but the rest of the officers and two hundred and eight men perished.

The 30th, order to hold ourselves in readiness to sail, and to ship cannons, mortars, and all necessary to make a regular siege. The same day we took on board our vessel the regiments of Gatinon, now Royal Auvergne, Agénois, Touraine, and a detachment of Lauzun's legion.

August. August 5th, all being ready, the signal was given to unmoor, and on the 6th, at 4, A. M., to loose sail. Our fleet numbered 24 vessels, and the wonder is that everybody, the English included, knew where we were going, while we had not even a conjecture as to the operation that our admiral was about to undertake.[1]

On the 7th the commander, de Glandevèse, who had sailed around the island to leeward, joined us with the *Bourgogne* and the *Hector*, which had been unable to set sail the day previous. The *Actionnaire*, which had come with the commander's five vessels, anchored on the 8th at the cape.

On the 10th the light squadron gave chase to the English frigate which had chased the *Fie* and forced her to put in at the Mole St. Nicolas, after she had fought three times; first with a frigate, which she sunk, next with a 50 gun vessel, which she cut up considerably by a manœuvre which excited the admi-

---

[1] The secret had been well kept, for a month before the Count de Grasse wrote to Rochambeau

ration of the enemy. She was then commanded by M. de Boubée, ensign[1], the captain having been killed in the first engagement. In the second action she lost her foremast. Her last affair was with the frigate of which I have just spoken, and which she would have taken, for all her crippled condition, had not the adversary's flight and superior sailing saved her. We learned that this young officer received general applause on his arrival at Cap François, having been crowned by a young and charming actress, who was the idol of that town, who then embraced him on the stage amid the acclamations of the spectators. He certainly deserved all the praise he received in this country. He had the pleasure of attaining the command of his frigate, which he took back to Brest, where he obtained another ship on which he sailed to India, by his own request. There he again distinguished himself in the last affair of the Bailly de Suffren, the French commander in that part of the world.

On the 11th we entered the old channel and took in a Spanish coast pilot coming from Baracao, a town lying on the northern coast of the island of Cuba. The passage of this channel is justly considered a very dangerous spot. We were so happy as to spend three days in the narrowest part of the pass, which is surrounded by reefs on every side, experiencing an unsupportable contrariety of winds. At length, on the

---

[1] In the French navy the ensign ranks next to the lieutenant

14th, a very strong wind sprang up, and we doubled the rocks, after suffering considerably. The *Northumberland* was almost lost, having got into the breakers very near the reefs, and being almost ungovernable through the fault of a helmsman, who gave the wheel a wrong turn.

At this period we flattered ourselves that we should behold the superb city of Havana, the capital of the island of Cuba, and the richest and strongest place in America; the Spaniards having added considerably to its fortifications since the last war. The *Aigrette* alone went there, and brought off four millions, which served as an excuse for the seventeen men of war there, not to accompany us on the expedition we had on hand. Is it not a shame for these vessels to lie rotting two years in port? It is only a nation as cowardly as the Spaniard that can wallow so in inaction, leaving its allies to bear all the brunt of the war.

On the 18th we lay to off Matanzas, three leagues from that town, and about thirty from Havana. We sent our pilots ashore, and entered the Bahama channel, into which the currents carried us. At this point, being in order, we learned that the projected expedition was to the Chesapeake. Here the charming maritime ill-temper displayed itself in all its beauty, for they closed the council-chamber door on the gentlemen of the Royal Auvergne, commanded by Mr. de Tourville, who could not help taking up the silly remarks they passed on the Count d'Estaing.

On the 24th we took three English vessels; one of which, commanded by . lieutenant in the navy, carried 16 six-pounders and 8 eighteen-pound howitzers. She had on board four officers and several young women, who, on passing into our hands, were greatly rejoiced at their adversity, and said that the French even on the sea were better than their countrymen. There is one style in which they surely would not prove it — being very knowing. I would willingly rely on their judgment, so far as their experience goes. The smaller of the other two was carrying to England a general officer[1] who had commanded at Savannah and Charleston, which he had left a week before, and who enjoyed the highest reputation. All these vessels, and those subsequently taken off this coast, were loaded with merchandise for Europe.

I cannot omit an incident which proves the bad faith with which the English are so justly reproached, an incident which they have often repeated In the evening, not having had time to man the prizes entirely, the enemy, to the number of sixty men, left in the larger vessel, found means during the night to open the *robinet* (a kind of port hole near the keel, used to let in water or to sink a vessel when she gets

---

[1] Lord Rawdon, retiring to England in ill health, after his barbarous and unjustifiable execution of Haines. He had now the mortification to witness, as a prisoner, the defeat of Cornwallis on land and Graves on the ocean

on fire, as Mr. du Plessis Pascault wished to do at the cape when the *Intrepide* caught fire). Fortunately this trick was discovered, and it was closed in time to prevent almost all damage. Had there been any delay in making the rounds, the vessel would to a certainty have gone down.

On the 28th the fleet anchored three leagues from the roadstead of the Chesapeake, according to the advice of the coast pilots whom we had on board. We had not yet seen any land, which here lies very low.

On the 29th we anchored in three columns, in the entrance of the roadstead,[1] after chasing a number of vessels that we could not make out. You will not perhaps be astonished to learn in what security the English live. Having anchored and displayed our flag, we were approached by a boat in which was one of the principal citizens of Virginia, who asked where Lord Rodney was. The sailors on deck hailed, and one of them, who spoke English well, told them to come on board, which they did at once. But what was their surprise to see only infantry in white uniforms. They were taken to the main cabin, where we were at dinner, and where the captain informed them that they were prisoners, ordering them to be well treated. The boat was taken, and found to contain excellent melons and many other refreshments, which were eaten in honor of Lord Rodney.

---

[1] In Lynn Haven Bay.

September. September 1st, our troops[1] got in boats and were landed without the slightest molestation from the forces composing the army of Lord Cornwallis, although he had a ship of the line, three frigates, and several small vessels. The English general might have prevented us from doing anything, and even repulsed us, had he not despised our small army. At our first encampment it would have been annihilated if attacked. Three days after, it formed a junction with the army of M. de la Fayette,[2] 1,800 strong, but who, at the same time, received a reinforcement of 1,800 more Americans, making in all 7,600. The English numbered 11,000 men. When told that the French had landed, their general merely remarked that he had been long expecting them, and was glad that they had come. For all that, he soon had reason to repent it.

That same day I almost perished in attempting to go ashore. The boat, that I was in, capsized, but, fortunately, the bar we struck on touched the land, and had scarcely four feet of water on it. I found

---

[1] This body consisted of 3,300 men, under the Marquis de St Simon, who were conveyed eighteen leagues up James river by the boats of the fleet, manned by 1,500 sailors. Cornwallis mentions, in his despatch to Clinton, the number of boats as forty, and of troops as 3,800 men. After landing these the boats transported Wayne's command.

[2] By this junction, Lafayette, at the age of 24, in his quality of major-general of the American army, had under his command a French general officer, the Marquis de St Simon.

this a magnificent country, with fine woods, houses at intervals, with little plains around; pasturages covered with immense herds of cattle of every kind; large river prodigiously full of fish. I put up at the house of the captain of an American frigate, who showed me every cordiality, and was kind enough to give our steward directions how to buy the stores which he knew our vessel must be in need of. In the evening I took my boat again to go aboard, but the tide and the currents were so violent that I was forced to anchor between the land and the fleet, about a league from each.

The 2d, the *Aigrette* arrived from the head of the bay with several prizes made by our different vessels, among others by the *Glorieux*, which gave chase to the *Charon*, of 50 guns, but could not get at her on account of the shoals, and which was burnt during the siege of Yorktown.

The 3d, four of our vessels were detached, and stationed at the mouths of the rivers, by which we took a considerable number of merchantmen. We were in the greatest impatience in consequence of the non-arrival of the *Concorde*, a frigate of M. du Barras'[1]

---

[1] Louis, Count de Barras St Laurent, born in Provence, had served long in the French navy, but his chief services were those in America He was a particular friend of the Count d'Estaing, and commanded his vanguard when he forced the entrance of Newport He reached Boston in May, 1781, in the *Concorde*, having been appointed to command the French squadron there He was then about 60 years old. Washington at once proposed an interview with him and Rochambeau

squadron, which was to announce to us the moment of the junction. In fact we did not know what to make of the delay; and some of the navy officers, jealous of his merit, accused him of being a bad citizen, and of being unwilling to serve under M. de Grasse, because he had, he said, his option to remain at Boston or join him. Already they wished to make him responsible for the blunders the admiral was to commit. In these circumstances M. de Barras will be seen giving a rare example of patriotism, which is unfortunately known only by name in France. We were in the greatest uncertainty as to what was to happen, when our two frigates on guard outside sig-

---

at Wethersfield, on the 22d of May, but as Arbuthnot appeared, the Count de Barras preferred not to be absent. He, however, through Rochambeau, objected to transporting the French army to the Chesapeake on his squadron, and subsequently declined to proceed to that bay with his vessels to prevent the escape of Cornwallis, and showed a reluctance to serve under de Grasse, his junior, proposing an expedition to Newfoundland. This, Washington at last induced him to abandon and coöperate in the general movement. He, however, projected an attack on the tory fort on Lloyd's neck, in July, which was a complete failure. He finally joined de Grasse, and materially aided in the reduction of Yorktown. From this, it will be seen that his yielding to serve under de Grasse was far from the noble sacrifice of feeling so often pretended. A warm partisan of d'Estaing, he was reluctant to contribute in any way to the success of his rival, and displayed a spirit of contrariety by no means exalting. After coöperating with de Grasse at the siege of Yorktown, he also took part in the engagement with Hood, off St. Christopher, on the 25-6 January, 1782; but after reducing Nevis and Monserrat, returned to France. He had considered de Grasse's promotion to the command of the fleet, and the rank of lieutenant-general, as a slight upon him. In the reorganization of the navy in 1782, he was made vice-admiral.

nailed sails in sight. These soon proved to be English, to the number of 21 men of war, two of them three deckers, and five frigates. As a combat was deemed certain, orders were given to hoist sail.

At half-past eleven, orders were given to slip our cables, and leaves the buoy; at noon, to clear decks and to form in order of speed. This, for a wonder, was pretty well executed, for every vessel had a hundred men in the boats, which had, as I have said, been landing our troops. The fleet formed in very bad order; for, to tell the truth, there were only four vessels in line, the *Pluto*, the *Bourgogne*, the *Marseillais*, and the *Diadême*. The *Refléchy* and the *Caton* came next, half a league to the lee of the first; and the rest of the fleet a league more to the lee of the latter, the *Ville de Paris* in the centre; the English were in the best possible order, bowsprit to stern, bearing down on us, and consequently to our windward. Admiral Graves commanded,[1] having under him rear-admirals Hood and Drake; they made an immense number of signals to each other before engaging us. The English vessel, the *Terrible*, which was pumping four pumps, not feeling in a condition to take part in the action, kept to the windward of the enemy's line,

---

[1] Graves commanded the *Sheerness* in 1757; in 1759, commanding the *Duke*, 90, he blockaded Brest. In 1781 he was in the *London*, 98. His engagement with de Grasse is here recorded. During the French revolution he served under Howe at Ouessant, May 5, 1794, and was wounded soon after in the *Royal Sovereign*. He was created a peer in June, 1794.

athwart Drake, who signalled her to take her position, which she lost some time in doing; but the rear-admiral soon persuaded her to take her place by sending her three cannon balls. Then it was that they tacked to the larboard as we did,[1] and hoisted a great white flag astern; but they soon struck it and hoisted their own. It was then five minutes after three, and the head of our line was within rifle shot; and, in fact, entirely separated from the rest of our fleet, a disagreeable position. Then they poured their first broadside into the *Refléchy*, killing the captain [2] That vessel soon bore away, as well as the *Cito*, on which they kept up a brisk fire Then Mr de Grasse signalled to the vessels, at the head of the line, to bear away two points, which was impracticable, as they were

---

[1] The English formed the line on the starboard tack, the French stood off shore on the larboard tack, but as Drake, who was in the rear, was signalled to bear down, the whole British fleet wore on the larboard tack The late Captain Ward, in his *Naval Tactics*, says "Admiral Graves bore down and attacked the French fleet by an oblique approach in column ahead, but in a manner which engaged the whole English line — the rear very distantly, though exposing the head of it most to the enemy's fire Hence the French, having inflicted far more injury than they received, wore round out of action, and reformed to leeward, for the purpose of again receiving the attack The English were not in condition to repeat it The English van ships on the approach, when only their bow guns bore, were exposed to a severe diagonal fire from the broadsides of the French van ships, as will appear by inspection of the figure, and this diagonal fire is nearly as destructive as a raking fire"

[2] The captain, killed in this action, according to Guérin, *Histoire de la Marine Française*, and the *Gazette de France*, was Brun de Boade, though our author, when he first mentions the *Refléchy* makes de Marigny captain of the *Refléchy*, de Boade commanded the *Triton*, 64, in 1780

fighting within gun-shot distance, and would have got a very severe handling, had they presented the stern. The four ships in the van found themselves, consequently, entirely cut off from the rest of the fleet, and constantly engaged with seven or eight vessels at close quarters; and the *Diadême* was constantly near Admiral Drake,[1] who set fire to her at every shot, the wadding entering her side. This vessel was constantly engaged with two and sometimes three vessels. The English would not cut off our van, which they might perhaps have taken, and which they would, at all events, have rendered past repair. They contented themselves simply with cutting up that part of our fleet which kept up a distant fight, the sailors of the *Ville de Paris* having been the last to take part in the action. Mr. de Bougainville commanded our van, but he was too far to leeward and in no condition to relieve the *Diadême*, which could scarcely hold out, and was on the point of boarding of the *Princesse*, commanded by the rear-admiral, who avoided her, then he turned all his fire on the *Terrible*, which he riddled, so that the English had to sink her next day. With all this, this vessel was utterly unable to keep up the fight, having only four thirty-six pounders and nine eighteens, fit for use, and having all on board

---

[1] Sir Francis Drake commanded the *Edgar* in 1759, was rear admiral at Gibraltar in April, 1781, with Graves at the Chesapeake and with Hood and Rodney in the West Indies, as described in these journals

killed, wounded or burnt. At this juncture M. de Chabert, commanding the *St. Esprit*, which had, for a long time, been engaged with the English admiral, and who was himself wounded, seeing the imminent danger of the *Diadême*, hoisted sail and was soon in her wake; then he opened a terrible fire, that the gentlemen of Albion could not stand, and had to haul their wind. The contest was kept up in the centre for half an hour longer. For our part we were so tired, that though within gun-shot, the vans no longer fired. At 6, the battle closed.[1]

---

[1] Admiral Graves says "As we approached, the whole fleet got under sail, and stretched out to sea, with the wind at north northeast. As we drew nearer I formed the line first ahead, and then in such a manner as to bring his majesty's fleet nearly parallel to the line of approach of the enemy, and when I found that our van was advanced as far as the shoal of the middle ground would admit of, I wore the fleet and brought them upon the same tack with the enemy, and nearly parallel to them, though we were by no means extended with their rear. So soon as I judged that our van would be able to operate, I made the signal to bear away and approach, and soon after to engage the enemy close. Somewhat after four the action began among the headmost ships, pretty close, and soon became general as far as the second ships from the centre towards the rear. The van of the enemy bore away to enable their centre to support them, or they would have been cut up. The action did not entirely cease until a little after sunset, though at a considerable distance, for the centre of the enemy continued to bear up as it advanced, and at that moment seemed to have little more in view than to shelter their own van as it went away before the wind. His majesty's fleet consisted of nineteen sail of the line—that of the French formed twenty-four sail in their line. After night I sent the frigates to the van and rear, to push forward the line and keep it extended with the enemy, with the full intention to renew the engagement in the morning. But when the frigate *Fortunée* returned from the van, I was informed that several of

In this affair we lost 400 men and 12 officers; the English came off with the loss of 700 men,[1] and many persons of distinction. We had to go to the assistance of the *Diadême* immediately after the battle, as she had lost 120 men and had no sails or rigging, having received 125 balls in her hull and 12 under the water line. We should have had to abandon her, had the sea run high, and do with her as the English did with the *Terrible*, 74. It is well to note that there were only 22 French vessels in this engagement, all badly manned. The enemy had 21 in line, one of 50 guns, and some frigates.

The English committed a great fault in this action. As soon as we left the roads of the Chesapeake, they should have entered and anchored. They were before the wind, and by hugging Cape Charles they might easily have moored with a spring in the cable, before we were formed in line and ready to attack them; this would leave us no alternative but to grapple them, otherwise our army would have run a great risk of being deprived of everything, perhaps have been captured even, our vessels, stationed at the York, Balti-

---

the ships had suffered so much, they were in no condition to renew the action until they had secured their masts. We, however, kept well extended with the enemy all night."

[1] Graves gives the loss at 90 killed and 246 wounded. The 1st lieutenant of the *Shrewsbury* was killed, and the captain wounded. The *Princess*, *Shrewsbury*, *Intrepide* and *Montague* suffered severely in the masts and the *Terrible* and *Ajax* in the hull. On the 10th he says a council of war determined to destroy the *Terrible*, and she was set fire to on the 11th.

more and James rivers, would have been taken, as well as all the boats of the fleet. Hood was in favor of running in here as we shall see him do at St. Christopher's, but Admiral Graves durst not. Another blunder that our enemies made was, their neglecting to cut off our four vessels at the head, which they might perhaps have taken, or at least cut off from the rest of the fleet.

There is no reproach to be made to Mr. de Grasse in this affair, except his not making in time the signals to take position in order of battle, and the blunder of not posting himself at the entrance of the bay and refusing fight. He committed a grosser blunder of this kind afterwards; for, on this occasion, he might allege the fact that he was waiting for Commodore de Barras, and that he exposed him prodigiously if he did not fight and force the enemy to open the entrance to the anchorage of the Chesapeake.

On the 6th we did not lose sight of the English, and the wind having varied slightly, by maneuvering a great deal, and the English little, we gained the weather-gage.

The 7th we still kept them in sight. On this day they sunk the *Terrible*. In the evening we lost sight of them; the sea beginning to run high and the wind increasing, our admiral made us steer for the Chesapeake. We did not, however, make Cape Henry till the 11th; and at the same time we saw two English frigates, the *Iris* and *Richmond*, each of 40 guns, chased by the *Glorieux*, as she was returning from the river. The *Aigrette* came up with the former and engaged her at pistol shot distance; but she had to haul off, she got so hardly used. Seeing that they held out so, several of our good sailors got at their heels; the rest of the fleet joined, and we poured in over two hundred balls before they struck. We made the Count de Barras, who had been at anchor in the roads for two days, start out two vessels of his division, as he could not make out which nation we belonged to. He had witnessed the affair of the 5th, but being unable to distinguish the French fleet, he had anchored in the roads where we found him. We dropped our anchors at six or seven in the evening, well satisfied with our prizes, and especially to get our boats again, which joined us this day, bringing back our best men

The 15th there came on board our fleet M. de Custine,[1] colonel of the regiment of Saintonge, commanding the van of General Washington's army, composed of a thousand French grenadiers, and as many American volunteers. He proceeded to join M. de la Fayette, and announced the speedy arrival of the combined armies of France and America, with all necessaries of war, and provisions, for our troops suffered for want of the latter

---

[1] Adam Philip, Count de Custine, born at Metz in 1740. He served under Frederick the Great in the Seven Years war. In 1792 he was summoned from the command of the army of the Rhine, to Paris, and beheaded in August, 1793

On the 18th the vessels bearing our soldiers arrived by Baltimore river, and the greater part of the army, coasting along, and bringing from Philadelphia all that was needed, and even more; for plenty always reigned in the camps, although this country has been completely devastated by the English. The American general came on board the *Ville de Paris*, where he had a long conference with Mr. de Grasse, and the other two naval commanders.[1] On his departure he was saluted with thirteen guns. He joined his army, 20,000 strong, including Rochambeau's and Lafayette's armies. I think that when Lord Cornwallis was told of Mr. Washington's arrival, he did not say, "so much the better," and must have laughed on the wrong side of his mouth.

The combined army having invested the English, they retired to Yorktown, posting a large detachment at Gloucester, a town on the other side of the river, and immediately opposite York. The enemy had already put these two places in a respectable state of defence, and four redouts protected the approaches. They thought proper, however, to evacuate the smaller

---

[1] "In company with Count de Rochambeau, the Chevalier de Chastelleux, General Knox and General Duportail, I set out for an interview with the admiral, and arrived on board the *Ville de Paris*, (off Cape Henry), the next day about noon, and having settled most points with him to my satisfaction, except not obtaining insurance of sending ships above York, I embarked on board the *Queen Charlotte*, the vessel I went down in; but by reason of hard blowing and contrary winds, I did not reach Williamsburgh again till the 22d." WASHINGTON's *Diary*.

two, which were, too, farther off. On the 20th Lord Cornwallis wished to cross the river, but was prevented by the fire of our frigates and other small craft, chiefly prizes taken on that coast. As the wind became very violent, Mr. de Grasse ran his fleet into the bay and anchored on a line, with springs on the cable. We all made our repairs then more at ease and got water more conveniently. It is worth remarking that we got it only by digging four or five feet in the sand. This country is so well wooded that I saw on board the *Diadême* a piece of timber costing 28 francs, measuring thirty feet long and twenty inches square. You may judge from this that we all made our repairs easily and without sparing.

On the 30th M. de Grasse disembarked 600 marines from the vessels to reinforce M. de Choisy's corps.[1] They repulsed the enemy, and compelled them to retire to Gloucester. The commanders had established such good communication that we heard from the camp every day, and were even near enough to see what was going on; for we witnessed the spectacle of the conflagration of an English 50 gun ship,[2] set on fire by the French battery.

October On the 18th of October Mr. de Barras was sent to the camp in the admiral's place, and took

---

[1] Mr de Choisy himself bore Washington's letter of request, which de Grasse granted reluctantly, desiring that no further requisition might be made. Sparks's *Washington*, VIII, 167 n

[2] The *Charon*

part in the capitulation of the positions of Yorktown and Gloucester, and of Lord Cornwallis's army, composed of 11,000 men, an army which had committed atrocities to the point even of killing a woman, opening her, taking out the child she bore in her womb, and hanging it to a tree, with this inscription: "Thou shalt not breed traitors."

This being the most brilliant conquest in the war, the capitulation cannot but be interesting. The readers will not be displeased to see the articles here:

Capitulation of Lord Cornwallis, on surrendering his posts of Yorktown and Gloucester and his army into the hands of General Washington, Lieut.-Gen. Count de Rochambeau, and Count de Grasse, lieut.-gen. commanding the naval forces of France in Chesapeake bay.

Article I.

The garrisons of York and Gloucester, including the officers and seamen of his Britannic Majesty's ships, as well as the mariners, to surrender themselves prisoners of war to the combined forces of America and France. The land troops to remain prisoners to the United States — the navy to the naval army of his Most Christian Majesty.

Granted

Article II.

The artillery, arms, accoutrements, military chest, and public stores of every denomination, shall be delivered unimpaired to the heads of departments appointed to receive them.

Granted.

Article III.

At twelve o'clock to-day the two redoubts on the left flank of York to be delivered, the one to a detachment of the American infantry, the other to a detachment of French grenadiers

Granted.

The garrison of York will march out to a place to be appointed in front of the posts, at two o'clock precisely, with shouldered arms, colors cased, and drums beating a British or German march. They are then to ground their arms, and return to their encampments, where they will remain until they are dispatched to the places of their destination Two works on the Gloucester side will be delivered at one o'clock to a detachment of French and American troops appointed to possess them. The garrison will march out at three o'clock in the afternoon; the cavalry with their swords drawn, trumpets sounding, and the infantry in the manner prescribed for the garrison of York. They are likewise to return to their encampments, until they can be finally marched off.

Article IV.

Officers are to retain their side arms. Both officers and soldiers to keep their private property of every kind; and no part of their baggage or papers to be at any time subject to search or inspection. The baggage and papers of officers and soldiers taken during the siege to be likewise preserved for them.

Granted.

It is understood that any property obviously belonging to the inhabitants of these states in the possession of the garrison, shall be subject to be reclaimed.

Article V.

The soldiers to be kept in Virginia, Maryland or Pennsylvania, and as much by regiments as possible, and supplied with the same rations of provisions as are allowed to soldiers in the service of America. A field officer from each nation, to wit, British, Anspach, and Hessian, and other officers on parole, in the proportion of one to fifty men, to be allowed to reside near their respective regiments, to visit them frequently, and be witnesses of their treatment, and that their officers may receive and deliver clothing and other necessaries for them, for which passports are to be granted when applied for.

Granted.

Article VI.

The general, staff, and other officers not employed, as mentioned in the above articles, and who choose it, to be permitted to go on parole to Europe, to New York, or to any other American maritime posts at present in the possession of the British forces, at their own option, and proper vessels to be granted by the Count de Grasse to carry them under flag of truce to New York within ten days from this date, if possible, and they to reside in a district to be agreed upon hereafter, until they embark.

The officers of the civil department of the army and navy to be included in this article. Passports to go by land to be granted to those to whom vessels cannot be furnished.

Granted.

Article VII.

Officers to be allowed to keep soldiers as servants, according to the common practice of the service. Servants not soldiers are not to be considered as prisoners, and are to be allowed to attend their masters.

Granted.

Article VIII.

The *Bonetta* sloop of war to be equipped and navigated by its present captain and crew, and left entirely at the disposal of Lord Cornwallis from the hour that the capitulation is signed, to receive an aid-de-camp to carry despatches to Sir Henry Clinton; and such soldiers as he may think proper to send to New York to be permitted to sail without examination. When his despatches are ready, his lordship engages on his part that the ship shall be delivered to the order of the Count de Grasse, if she escapes the dangers of the sea. That she shall not carry off any public stores.

Any part of the crew that may be deficient on her return, and the soldiers passengers, to be accounted for on her delivery.

Article IX.

The traders are to preserve their property, and to be allowed three months to dispose of or remove them, and those traders are not to be considered as prisoners of war.

The traders will be allowed to dispose of their effects, the allied army having the right of preëmption. The traders are to be considered as prisoners of war upon parole.

Article X.

Natives or inhabitants of different parts of this country at present in York or Gloucester, are not to be punished on account of having joined the British army.

This article cannot be assented to, being altogether of civil resort.

Article XI.

Proper hospitals to be furnished for the sick and wounded. They are to be attended by their own surgeons on parole; and they are to be furnished with medicines and stores from the American hospitals.

The hospital stores now in York and Gloucester shall be delivered for the use of the British sick and wounded. Passports will be granted for procuring them further supplies from New York, as occasion may require; and proper hospitals will be furnished for the reception of the sick and wounded of the two garrisons.

Article XII.

Wagons to be furnished to carry the baggage of the officers attending the soldiers, and to surgeons when traveling on account of the sick, attending the hospitals at public expense.

They are to be furnished, if possible.

Article XIII

The shipping and boats in the two harbors, with all their stores, guns, tackling and apparel, shall be delivered up in their present state to an officer of the navy appointed to take possession of them, previously unloading the private property, part of which had been on board for security during the siege.

Granted.

Article XIV.

No article of capitulation to be infringed on pretense of reprisals, and if there be any doubtful expressions on it, they are to be interpreted according to the common meaning and acceptation of the words.

Granted.

Done at Yorktown, Virginia, October 19, 1781.

CORNWALLIS,
THOS SYMONDS.

Done in the trench, before Yorktown in Virginia, October 19, 1781.

    G. WASHINGTON,
    LE COMTE DE ROCHAMBEAU,
    LE COMTE DE BARRAS.

En mon nom et celui du
    COMTE DE GRASSE

DIVISION OF THE COUNT DE BARRAS.

The Duc de Bourgoyne,	80 guns,	Count de Barras.
Neptune	74	Destouches.
Conquérant	74	La Grandière
Ardent	66	de Marigny.
Eveillé	64	de Tilly.
Provence	64	de Lombard
Jason	64	de la Clocheterie.
Romulus	50	Villebrune.

The 27th we were engaged in reëmbarking our troops, artillery, and munitions of war, and the same day the English hove in sight off the head of the roads, to the number of 31 sail. Two frigates were stationed there, and a third went out to examine. She returned next day and reported to the admiral that 41 English vessels were cruising outside, several of them being frigates, and smaller craft. M. de Grasse would not budge with his fleet.[1] We have learned that Prince William,[2] son of King George, was in the fleet, which he had joined with three vessels from England within a few days.

On the 30th the enemy were again signalled, and we felt sure of having another action with them in those waters; and the reason of our not engaging them, is, doubtless, the violent winds which blew for several days. The admiral profited by their departure to send two frigates to France with his despatches and those of the generals of the troops, which cannot have been received with indifference. One division of the fleet was intended to go to Cape François, and the regiment of Gatinois, now Royal Auvergné,[3] was sent

---

[1] The second journal correctly states that De Grasse, in so doing, deferred to the express request of Washington.

[2] The late King William IV of England and Hanover.

[3] The regiment of Gatinois was, says Soulés, made up from the regiment of Auvergne, and was to lead the attack. The Count de Rochambeau said to the grenadiers· My boys, if I need you to-night I

on board them so as to be conveyed to that capital, where a considerable convoy has assembled to be escorted to Europe by M. D'Albert St. Hippolite.¹ These vessels are the *Victoire, Vaillant, Triton, Provence* and *Hector*. The last, by a blunder common enough in fleets, instead of following her destination, rejoined us, her captain, by name Dalins, intentionally misunderstanding what had just been hailed to him from a small royal brig. Moreover, this officer wished to serve, and was sure of soon having another vessel, for the *Hector* was good for nothing. In fact, on reaching Martinique, he got the command of the *Neptune*, which drew out much complaint from several captains his seniors in the service.

Before leaving this country I wish to say something of North America and its people. The Americans are generally large, strong and well made; the women are handsome, tapering in form, have very little bust, of a disposition the more gentle from the fact of their having among them many Anabaptists, known to be

---

hope you will not forget *Auvergne sans tache,* an honorable epithet of this regiment, which it has merited on all occasions. They replied that they would be killed to a man, and at the same time asked to have their old name restored. They behaved so as to deserve the highest praise; and the king has since, by an ordinance, given this regiment the name of Royal Auvergne.—*Troubles de l'Amér Ang*, III, 395.

¹ De Grasse was at this time anchored within the Horse Shoe, and according to Robin, could not have prevented a landing by Clinton But that author, like the writer of this journal, censures De Grasse unjustly. The succeeding journal states correctly that De Grasse yielded to the express request of Washington

most charitable of all sects. Hospitality is greatly practiced, as travelers in this extensive country are few, scarcely any in fact. The servants are negroes, certainly the least unhappy of their kind, being treated with more kindness than our lackeys are in France; hence we never hear in this country of masters poisoned by their negroes, so common an occurrence in our West India islands. The Anglican is the dominant religion; all are suffered there; the language is English. I believe these two things may well make them give the English the preference over us in a few years. The Americans are phlegmatic, extremely serious, always engaged in their business, and that of the state. They are with their wives only to take tea or some other drink. The girls are very free, and can have a lover without their parents finding it amiss; but if they are unfortunate enough to have a child, they must leave the country, unless they get married; but woe to the stranger who in such cases refuses to marry, for he refuses at the risk of his life. The women are as reserved as the girls are unreserved, and I do not think that unfaithful ones can be cited; at all events they behave with the greatest reserve: yet they were very fond of the French officers, whom they preferred even to their countrymen, but with all possible decency. This is perhaps the only country where justice is known and rendered. I saw an American, taken in arms among the English, punished with death because he had taken the oath of fidelity to the congress; and others in the same condition were merely treated as prisoners of war, because they had always served the Royalist party.

America is intersected by very large rivers. It is still covered with wood, and has many marshes. For this reason, at the same latitude, it is much colder than in Europe. This country produces ship timber, which would be excellent for the largest vessels; it abounds in cattle of all kinds, the flesh being fully equal to that of ours in Europe. These articles constitute their staples of trade. The productions of this country are absolutely the same as ours, except Indian corn, which they make into bread, and rice, which they also cultivate. The birds, game and fish are entirely different from ours. The Americans are much given to bartering; hence in several districts, especially in Virginia, they preferred sugar, ratafia, brandy, linen, cloth and leather to money, and gave us in exchange tobacco, and in the north, furs.

November November 4th the fleet weighed anchor; the *Zelé* and *Conquerant* touched on a sand bank, called Middleground. They ploughed through it so that the progress of the fleet was not retarded by this event. When two leagues south of Cape Henry the frigates on the look out signalled sails to the leeward, but the admiral would not let us give chase, the wind and sea being very high.

On the 5th and 6th vessels were again signalled, and we gave chase in vain, although the admiral's orders were to come to action as soon as possible.

On the 8th the vessels intended for the cape parted from the fleet and steered for St. Domingo, while we held on our way to Martinique, with good wind, a little too strong, and a frightful sea.

On the morning of the 9th the *Hector* rejoined us, her captain having pretended to misunderstand the admiral's order, which was communicated to him by the officer commanding a brig, the bearer of Mr. De Grasse's orders. That same day 18 sail were signalled to our windward, which made us sail close to the wind; but after two hours useless chase, we resumed our route with forced winds.

On the 11th and 12th we experienced the most disagreeable thing felt at sea; for the wind having suddenly fallen, and the sea still very rough, the vessels pitched so violently that we expected our masts to go over every moment, and we all but lost our mainmast, as a small vessel actually did.

On the 13th the wind sprang up again and from a good quarter. Mr. de Grasse made us resume our route, to the sound of thunder, which still muttered in the distance. Thus the day passed. About six in the afternoon the wind increased considerably, and the storm overtook us with fearful and repeated flashes of lightning. The nearest land was St. Domingo, two hundred and fifty leagues off. This lasted till eight o'clock, when we found ourselves in the midst of a violent tempest, the night very dark, the heavens on fire, the wind fearful and the sea furious — this with such violent peals of thunder that most of the vessels could not hear the admiral's signals, though given with heavy cannon, for thus far we have continued our route, and Mr. de Grasse ought to have had his fleet dispersed, but he still had the right to commit faults without being compelled to regret it. We lay to starboard to the wind. Scarcely was this manœuvre completed than there came two fearful claps of thunder, the clouds opened, inundating us, the wind redoubled, and I do not see how some of the vessels escaped being swamped (that is to say, have half the ship under water and be ready to capsize). We took necessary precautions to avert the most imminent accidents, all the crews were up and at work, and in the deepest silence. This agreeable weather lasted till two o'clock in the morning. The rest of the night was stormy, and at six the tempest ceased, to the great delight of all parties interested. The lightning struck the *Richemont*, without injuring the vessel, but killing two men and wounding three.

On the 15th we saw a water-spout, a very considerable mass of air and water in the form of a truncated cone, which pumps up the sea till the volume of water outweighs that of air, when it bursts. The volume of a spout, as I was assured by several intelligent seamen, is enough to swamp the largest vessels. We fired two cannon balls at it, to break it, but did not succeed, as we were too far off.

On the 21st the brig *Cornwallis* went ahead to announce our arrival to the Marquis de Bouillé, at Fort Royal.

On the 25th we hove in sight of the Morne du Vauclin. Order to crowd sail, so as to make the anchorage of Martinique. The fleet did not clear decks to pass the channel of St Lucia; on the contrary, I never saw it go with such fancied security and such disorder, for the first and last vessels were at least five leagues apart, so that two-thirds anchored on the 25th, while the rest could not come to anchor before the next day. Most assuredly, in this disorder, ten English vessels would have given us our hands full. We were in hopes to find in the roads some vessels from France, with a convoy; but our hopes were fallacious, and we, as well as the colony, were on the verge of running out of provisions.

We were greatly surprised, on arriving at Fort Royal, to learn the departure of the Marquis de Bouillé with 1500 men, on two frigates and all the boats or domains, on an expedition to which no one had any clue.

December On the 1st we learned that he had just taken St. Eustatius, a Dutch emporium which Rodney had captured, as I stated on our arrival at the West Indies. To recover this colony, he used one of those bold stratagems that always succeed with a man of talent who has won the affection of his troops. The Marquis de Bouillé knew how negligently the English lay at St. Eustatius, and first landed Dillon's regiment,[1] which, in red coats, and speaking English, could better cover the design. Four hundred soldiers of this regiment were disembarked at three o'clock; the sea, which was running very high, prevented the landing of the rest. A hundred men of Walsh's regiment had landed on another side, commanded by Mr O'Conor.[2] Imagining that he heard the signal, he marched straight on the fort, but was much surprised to see, instead of his fellow-soldiers of Dillon's regiment, the English recruits at drill. He

---

[1] This regiment formed part of the celebrated Irish brigade in the French service, originally composed of the Irish forces who defended Limerick for James II, and on its surrender were left to choose either the French or English service. They fortunately chose the former, as the English government absolved itself from the moral obligation of keeping the treaty. This brigade was maintained till the French revolution, and distinguished itself greatly at Fontenoy and other battles During the American revolution, regiments of the Irish brigade served at Savannah and in the West Indies. The recruiting for this brigade was kept up in Ireland in spite of heavy penalties, and the recruits were termed wild geese On the present occasion only Count Dillon and 50 chasseurs of his regiment were able to land; the other boats were broken on the rocks and many lives lost, but the Marquis de Bouillé, whose own boat capsized, found a less dangerous spot, and disembarked the rest rapidly

[2] The Marquis styles this officer the "Chevalier O'Connor, Captain of Walsh's Chasseurs," but makes Dillon attack the troops on parade I do not find this Capt O'Connor on any list at hand. There was, however, a Major O'Conor in Dillon's regiment in 1789, *de Waroquier, Etat Général* The Chevalier John Keating, probably the last survivor of this regiment, Walsh-Serrant, died a few years since in Philadelphia, aged 96

fired on them at once; they fled into the fort, and he after them up to the gate, which he seized. The French troops came up in a moment, rushed in, and compelled the English to capitulate in their quarters, breeches in hand. Mr. O'Conor went and arrested the governor, who, taking him for an officer of his garrison, scolded him for the firing and the trouble among the troops, but was much amazed when informed that his interlocutor was French, and himself a prisoner of his Most Christian Majesty. He went to the window to look, and fell back fainting when he saw the regiment of Auxerrois drawn up in line of battle on the square, and Mr. de Bouillé giving orders. He then repented of the party of pleasure in the country to which he had just been, and from which he got back two hours before the surprise. The garrison, to the number of 756, were taken prisoners of war. Four million livres were taken; 170,000 belonging to Rodney or his troops, arising from the booty taken by the English, were distributed among the troops engaged in this expedition, and the rest was restored to the Dutch colonists. St. Martin and Anguilla were also taken, and all was restored to the condition of things before the arrival of the enemy.[1]

---

[1] James Cockburne, lieut. col of the 35th foot and governor of St Eustatia, was tried by court martial and found "guilty of culpable neglect in not taking the necessary precautions for the defence of the island, notwithstanding he had received the fullest intelligence of an intended attack." The better accounts make Cockburne captured on the parade with the troops

There was nothing interesting during our stay at Martinique; the repeated visits of an English frigate which came and reconnoitred us every other day,[1] and which we made no attempt to take or chase, was the only thing that occurred. The arrival of the Marquis de Bouillé and his little division, out of which he had left a strong garrison at St. Eustatius, occupied us more than that of sixteen English vessels at the windward isles.

On the 17th we set sail again, steering through the St. Lucia channel. The sea ran mountain high; I never saw it so high without a strong wind. In the evening the *Destin* had to put back, having met with an accident in her masts. We also saw small whales.

The 18th is remarkable for the collision of the *Solitaire* and *Conquérant*, the latter went to Fort Royal to refit; as for the *Solitaire*, which lost her bowsprit and foremast, she was unable to make Fort Royal, and was forced to put in at Cape François. It is strange to see so many collisions and no punishment; it is very astonishing that there was not a council of war, and it was absolutely necessary. We shall see in the sequel how injurious these collisions were, and what they brought on our fleet, and what they cost M. de Grasse. The sea being frightful and the wind too

---

[1] The English naval commanders kept so sharp an eye on the French, that we have a report, dated Nov. 30, 1781, by Capt John M Laurin of the *Triton*, describing quite minutely the twenty-eight vessels of De Grasse's fleet as they lay at anchor at Fort Royal.

strong to run up the channel, we put back again the 23d, having the most of our vessels to unrig.

On the 26th we took the troops on board, and the 27th we sailed, leaving the division of the Count de Barras in port. We proposed to take Barbadoes, while that commander was taking St. Christopher's, where we were to join him. It was, I think, very ill-calculated; but as the wind did not allow our running up the channel of St. Lucia, where we suffered terribly, we were brought back to the anchorage, a thing we needed greatly.

January, 1782

On the 4th of January, 1782, the fleet anchored at Fort Royal, and left on the 5th with the division that had remained there, except the *Caton* and *Lion Brittanique* (a transport taken from the English), carrying our field artillery, which anchored at St. Eustatius. We steered to St. Christopher's, experiencing calms and much fog.

On the 7th, being under Guadaloupe, the fleet separated, and rejoined on the 8th.

On the 10th the *Sceptre* and the *Glorieux* gave chase to an English 74, which they would have taken if the admiral had not obliged them to return to their posts.

On the 11th the fleet anchored at the Basse Terre, St. Christopher's, after destroying and dismounting several batteries.

On the 13th the *Duc de Bourgoyne*, the *Diadême*, the *Zélé* and the separated vessels joined us, as well as the *Caton*, which arrived from St Eustatius. The whole island surrendered the 12th, the inhabitants having capitulated for themselves and for Nevis. The troops landed without the least opposition. Fort Brimstone Hill, the only important place, but susceptible of a vigorous defence, was the refuge of the garrison, which prepared to make vigorous efforts to preserve the island. Sir Thomas Shirley, governor of the windward isles, and Sir Thomas Frazer, were in the redoubt, resolved to defend the position as long as possible. They were, moreover, confident that they could not be taken, and so the English engineers assured them. We found in the different ports of that island fifty vessels, which we took.

On the 12th M. de Bouillé and his army were under Brimstone Hill or the redoubt, and at once began his preparations for an attack. A 50 gun ship and two frigates were posted to blockade the port, and M. Descars, commanding the *Glorieux*, proceeded to sweep off several vessels moored under the redoubt.

The 13th our troops had well nigh lost their general; 50 negroes from the houses near Brimstone Hill having fired on him while reconnoitering. The 14th these houses were burned. M. de Grasse felt some uneasiness about the *Destin*, but learned that she had put back to Fort Royal in consequence of her leaking badly. The *Lion Britannique* has just been lost on St. Christopher's by the awkwardness of the creole who commanded it, and who had no merit but the protection of the commanders. All was saved, though the mortars would have gone down but for the plan adopted by an artillery officer. The vessel was a total wreck.

3d Engagement. 1st of St. Christopher's. On the 22d we learned that the English were under sail, coming to the relief of the colony, having a fleet to the windward of 22 vessels, two of them three deckers, commanded by Admiral Hood. Ours, to the number of 28, hoisted sail on the evening of the 23d. That same night we got an exact report of the enemy, and at noon on the 24th we discovered them off Rhidon, doubling that little isle, under which they lay to, with an air of hesitation. M. de Grasse also lay to and committed the blunder of waiting for them; but he had forgotten that the enemy, being to the windward, would always retain the advantage, and that he could not approach them at the same angle as they did us, enabling them to enter the anchorage in spite of our fleet. The decks had long been cleared for action. The light squadron, commanded by Mr. de Montenil, was ordered to hug the point of Isle Nevis. This was very badly executed; at least it was supposed that that officer acted intentionally, knowing that he had received many slights from Mr. de Grasse, who by a trick deprived him of the command of the *Languedoc*, 80, and gave him that of the *Ardent*, 66, which was rotten and was to take him back to France; but at the moment of action he carried his flag to the *Nep-*

tune, one of the vessels of his division.[1] Admiral Hood, seeing our fleet retire from Nevis and fall to leeward, made his advance under light sail and in excellent order. Mr. de Grasse signalled his fleet to crowd sail, keeping the wind on the larboard tack. He soon after poured half a broadside on the enemy; but the balls did not reach, and we did not get fairly within gun shot till half an hour later, about half past three. The *Glorieux*, *Sceptre*, *Ville de Paris*, and some others, brought the enemy to close action. The *Sceptre* received many balls, but fortunately very few of them went through or did much harm. In spite of our fire, the English admiral managed his fleet so well that it anchored in our place with a spring on the cable, under our fire, without Mr. de Grasse preventing them. The four rear vessels of the English fleet were indeed badly handled, and it was even pretended that we should have taken two of them. Mr. de Barras, who was in our rear division, was cannonaded by that of the English for a long time, followed by only two vessels, but, on the signal to veer off in order, we left the enemy to anchor at their ease. At 6 the combat ended, and we kept on broadside to broadside all

---

[1] The other account ascribes the same misconduct to Monteil, giving details which leave no doubt that this officer was guilty of a most criminal disobedience of orders in an actual engagement with the enemy. It gives a sad idea of the state of insubordination reigning in the fleet. In the English navy such conduct would have been punished with death, as it enabled Hood to escape John Rodney, and thus bring on the French fleet one of the most disastrous defeats in its annals.

night long, so as to get to windward. Our faults are too evident to require any pointing them out.[1] An English frigate was burnt under Nevis by the crew for fear of falling into our hands.

4th Engagement. 2d of St Christopher's
On the 25th at daybreak, signal to make ready for action; we were then beyond Nevis. Soon after, signal to form in line of battle in inverse order, and to the *Souverain*, commanded by Mr. de Glandeve, to take the head of the line. At 8, order to concentrate on the English rear division. At 9¾ we began the action; but in consequence of the good will and affection entertained for the admiral, all efforts were turned to the centre of the fleet. However we were fortunate enough, and our gunners expert enough, to handle the four rear vessels in the English line so severely that they were forced to weigh anchor under our fire, and could hardly have been more cut up than they were. As our ships passed the last English vessels they veered in the same order. This action was simply a brush, which lasted two hours, and amounted to nothing, our fleet always keeping to windward.

5th Engagement. 3d of St. Christopher's
At 3 o'clock, signal to clear for action and to come to close action with the rear. This was done at 4; and we so harrassed

---

[1] Commander Ward, in his *Naval Tactics*, says that De Grasse's error was in anchoring near into the shore with both extremities of his line exposed. They compelled him to sail out, in hopes of drawing Hood out, but the latter anchored on the outer edge of the anchorage, with his leading vessel under a point of land, and his rear protected by vessels between the line and the shore

the English rear that Admiral Hood replaced the four rear vessels by others which had suffered less in the three engagements, supposing that he would have to fight two battles a day for some time to come. Our fleet lost 2 or 300 men in these affairs,[1] and four officers; the enemy lost more, and besides lost all their wounded. The French fleet always under sail, hugging the wind, which it sometimes lost; the English fleet still anchored with springs on the cables, always with decks cleared for action, and ready to begin. So we rode for 19 days.

On the 28th, several of our vessels needed provisions. The admiral ordered those who had any left to share with those which had run out. The English that day landed 1200 men,[2] who were repulsed with considerable loss by M. de Fléchin, who had under him only 274 men of the regiments of Agenois and Touraine. They were compelled to reembark, which they did under the fire of their frigates or ships. This action certainly does great honor to the French infantry, and proves its superiority over the English.

On the 31st, the *Cornwallis* and the frigate *Astrée* joined our fleet, and we learned that several vessels, loaded with flour from New England, had reached Fort Royal.

---

[1] Gordon gives the English loss at 72 killed, 241 wounded

[2] These were troops from Antigua, under General Prescott, and the 69th regiment. Gordon's version of the affair is very different. He makes them repulse the French with loss, and finally retire to the ships without losing a man

February. On the 2d, at 4 P. M., the Marquis de Vaudreuil,[1] commodore commanding the *Tri-*

---

[1] The family of Vaudreuil figure so frequently in our history, in various places, as governors of Canada, of Montreal, Three Rivers, Louisiana, St Domingo, as commodores and captains in the navy, that in the French loose way of styling an officer, simply "M. de Vaudreuil," one member is often confounded with another. The most distinguished are. 1. Philip de Rigaud, Marquis de Vaudreuil, who died at Quebec, Oct. 10, 1725, after having been for 21 years governor of Canada and lieutenant-general of New France. 2 His son Louis Philippe de Rigaud, Count de Vaudreuil, who became ensign of marines (Troupes de la Marine), March 2, 1698; lieutenant in 1701, captain in 1710, ensign of a ship of the line in 1711; lieutenant of same, 1713, captain of same, 1738, in this capacity he commanded the *Intrépide* in the action between Vice-Admiral Hawke and M de l'Estenduere, Oct 25, 1747. He was created commodore in 1748, lieutenant-general of the naval forces in 1753; and died at Tours in 1763 By his wife, Catharine Le Moyne de Séregny, a niece of Iberville, he had: 3 Louis Philippe Rigaud, Marquis de Vaudreuil, born at Rochefort, Oct 28, 1724, entered the navy in 1740, was with his father in the *Intrépide*, lieutenant on the *Arethusa*, when taken, in 1754; captain of a frigate in 1764, of a ship of the line in 1765, commanded the *Fendant*, 74, at the battle of Ouessant, July 27, 1778 After reducing Senegal with a squadron, in 1779, he joined d Estaing in the West Indies, on the 21st of April, though with crews thinned by African fevers In the action off Granada, July 6, 1779, he opened the battle with the *Fendant*, and was the last to cease firing as Biron drew off He was apparently at the siege of Savannah, and the next year, still in the *Fendant*, distinguished himself in the battle of Martinique, April 17, between de Guichen and Rodney After taking part in the engagement between de Guichen and Kempenfeld, he sailed in the *Triomphant* to the West Indies. His career under the Count de Grasse will be found in these pages After the defeat of De Grasse, he drew off the rest of the fleet and proceeded to Boston, where he formed a project to attack the English in Maine, and after dispatching La Pérouse to Hudson's Bay, sailed to the West Indies, in 1783, to join in the attack on Jamaica, and was at Porto Cabello when news of peace arrived He then returned to France in the *Northumberland*. He was subsequently lieutenant-general of the naval forces In 1789 he was deputy of the nobles of Castelnaudry, and in 1791 he retired to England, but returned

omphant, 80, joined us, with M. d'Amblimont in the *Brave*, 74. The next day they approached the English, and M. de Vaudreuil found their position respectable.

On the 11th we learned that M. de Grasse had wished to raise the siege of St. Kitts; Mr. de Bouillé retained him by firmness. We were told, moreover, that it was simply the admiral's personal dissatisfaction with his captains that had induced him to take this false step.

On the 5th several frigates supplied such of the vessels as needed provisions, and then only we heard the misfortune that had befallen M. de Guichen, and the delay of the convoy that was so sorely needed.

On the 6th the *Cornwallis* took a schooner of six guns, which kept constantly plying between the enemy's fleet and Nevis to get fresh provisions; the English not daring to land at St. Kitts, which was guarded by our troops.

On the 8th the *Richemont* brought us some small vessels loaded with provisions, as well as the *Resolu*, which had already taken to the camp the third battalion of the regiment of Haynault.

On the 9th the English set fire to a merchantman, which they cast off, and which did not burn down till next day. That same day the English sent a small boat and a sloop, with a flag, to ask the admiral to

---

and died at Paris, December 14, 1802 4 His brother Louis de Rigaud, Chevalier de Vaudreuil, also mentioned in these pages, was born in 1728; ensign of a ship of the line in 1746, lieutenant in 1756, captain of a frigate in 1764

allow a transport with two hundred wounded to pass through to one of their islands, which was refused.

On the 11th, arrived a Spanish packet. An officer from her boarded the *Ville de Paris*, and after a long conference with the admiral, sailed for the Leeward Isles. The day but one before, an officer commanding a brig bearing dispatches to the admiral, carried them to Admiral Hood, mistaking one nation for the other; and in fact he might expect to find the English standing off and the French at anchor, knowing that we were besieging St. Kitts.

Surrender of St. Kitts and Nevis. On the 12th, to the great joy of all, we saw a white flag raised on the breach of the redoubt. We could scarcely believe our eyes: for the toil and hardship that de Bouillé's army had to undergo are incredible; and men must love a commander to suffer the severe duty imposed on 7000 men doing that of 21000. There were officers and men who slept only one night under their tents during the whole siege, which was most interesting from the manner in which it was begun, conducted, and especially terminated.

On the 13th Mr. de Grasse safely made his fleet anchor under Nevis, to take in provisions from transports that had anchored at St. Eustatius the day before, and which had come to Nevis; an operation that could have been performed under sail. We accordingly anchored three leagues to the windward of the English, without a single frigate on the lookout. Mr. de

Vaudreuil anchored as near the enemy as possible, so as to observe their movements; but we shall see Mr. Hood walk off without being in the least interfered with.

On the 14th we took in provisions. At night the English admiral kindled on shore fires corresponding to those carried at the poop by the commanders of the three divisions of his fleet. He cut his cables and started, leaving Mr. de Grasse at his anchorage, who the next day opened his eyes to see the English, and discovered only the coast; but he perceived the tops of their masts about three leagues off. So afraid were we of molesting them that we did not even send a paltry corvette to see them take their final departure from this quarter. The people of St. Kitts had very justly remarked, that those who knew so well how to get in would know how to get out. Yet here was a French admiral in command of the largest fleet in America for nineteen months.

On the 15th we reoccupied our old anchorage at the Basse Terre, St. Kitts, to reembark the troops, ammunition, arms and prisoners. I profited by this delay to visit the island, which is the finest, most valuable and best cultivated of the Windward Isles. The people are mild and upright, and what is extraordinary in this country, they are moral. It must be admitted that the English are the nation who do best in the West Indies; and in fact we would do well to go and take a few lessons from these haughty islanders. I saw the trenches of the French general opened under the enemy's nose, and went up to Brimstone Hill. Two roads lead to the summit of this morne, fortified with a triple work on two-thirds of the circumference; the first is a kind of *fausse bray*, all divided into curtains and bastions, or demi-bastions, well mounted with artillery, even large cannon and mortars. The interior is full of elevations, which command each other. The works were not much beaten down, when three thousand men capitulated after three weeks open trenches.

On the 17th the frigate *Aigrette* took a vessel carrying two hundred wounded English, badly supplied with provisions. If she had been kept long at sea, the poor fellows would certainly have died of hunger or jumped overboard. This is a specimen of English humanity.

On the 19th the *Aigrette* left for France with dispatches from the two commanders, which were certainly received in a very different manner.

Capture of Monserrat On the 20th we hoisted sail and steered for Martinique. The 22d and 23d were spent in taking Monserrat and in deciding the lot of the inhabitants. M. de Barras was employed on this little expedition, during which we were lying to under the island.

On the 26th at 8 A. M., the fleet anchored at Fort Royal, Martinique. Each vessel did its best to refit; an operation which was badly done, the colony being destitute of everything. During our stay in this roadstead we had, as usual, the repeated visit of an English frigate. Their fleet arrived at St. Lucia without any opposition from us, and Lord Rodney also arrived there with seven vessels from Europe, having left his convoy at Barbadoes. Several vessels from France reached us too, commanded by Mr. Mitton, who brought us the long desired convoy, and was very near being taken by the English as he came to land. The commanders received by these vessels orders to celebrate a double holiday, for the birth of the dauphin, and for the capture of Yorktown.

The first fête was given by General de Bouillé. All the genteel people of Martinique were invited. At the morning gun all the vessels were dressed with flags (which is done by fastening to the rigging all the flags on board, so as to form certain designs). Nightfall was the time when the *Te Deum* was chanted. Three thousand men were under arms, and the troops at Fort Bourbon formed a group on the ramparts, which, lighted up by the musketry and artillery, was very fine. The infantry began by a general discharge, followed by all the artillery of the fort, answered by the fleet, each vessel firing 21 guns. There were three successive discharges in the same way. All the people assembled on the savannah or square, where some poor fireworks were set off, which the people of the island thought very fine. The city was illuminated; the government house with great taste. All the better class who were invited to the ball proceeded to the general's. M. de Grasse and Mme. de Bouillé opened it. It was very brilliant in point of numbers and dress, but not in matter of beauty; for the creole women are all ugly, with the yellow complexion of the country. They are, too, very ill mannered. Accustomed to speak to their slaves, they have a certain tone which they can never drop, with no education either, unless they have been to France, which they leave reluctantly after spending some time there.

A broad path in M. de Bouillé's garden was tented over; plates set for one hundred and twenty; a hundred lighted tapers formed within the tent scattered groups, the effect of which was pleasing. All the seats except six were taken by women, who ate like ogres, and who, after filling their stomachs, filled their pockets also, and did it with the more gusto, as all on the table was excellent. A truce was put to their pleasures for half an hour, after which the ball recommenced, not, however, to last long, for at three o'clock there was no one left except the gamesters, who did not retire till eight. This is the country where gaming is most in vogue; every one plays, and what is more, plays high. I saw several parties where nothing but *les portugaises* were played.

The next day a frigate came from St. Lucia under a white flag, bringing fifty prisoners, who were exchanged. Rodney, Hood, and several English officers, sent delicacies to M. de Grasse, de Vaudreuil, and others, and we sent in return some of the liquors of the Widow Amphousse of Martinique, which they prize highly. The admiral begged the commander of the frigate to tell Mr. Rodney that he invited him and the officers of his fleet to come and participate in the festivities and pleasures going on in the colony, and that he would send passports. The merchants of St. Pierre gave splendid entertainments, and after them M. de Grasse gave his, which was like M. de Bouillé's, except that the women were a little coarser, and stuffed their pockets more; for they carried off bottles of liquor, one of which breaking in a beauty's pocket, she fled from the ball room, more annoyed at her dress being spoiled than at the odor diffused by the liquor. The officers laughed heartily, but the women, who feared, perhaps, that the same might happen to themselves, commisserated her loudly.

The French and English fleets having greatly increased, it will doubtless be agreeable to see at a glance their respective forces. The engagements of April 9 and 12 are of sufficient interest to give the names of the vessels and captains of the two nations who took part in this action.

STATE OF THE ENGLISH FLEET IN THE ENGAGEMENTS,
APRIL 9 AND 12, 1782.

Vessel.	Force.	Commanded by
Formidable,	98	Admiral Rodney.
Namur,	90	Fanshaw.
Prince George,	98	Balfour.[1]
Duke,	90	Sir Samuel Hood.[2]
Barfleur,	90	Hood.[3]
Conqueror,	74	Balfour.
Fame,	74	Barber.
Arrogant,	74	Cornish.
Hercules,	74	Savage.
Marlborough,	74	Penny.
Anson,	64	Blair.
Prothee,	64	Buckner
Yarmouth,	64	Parry.
Nonsuch,	64	Truscott.
Warrior,	74	Sir James Wallace.
Princess,	74	Samuel Drake.
Bedford,	74	Commodore Affleck.
Centaur,	74	Inglefield.
Ajax,	74	Charrington.
Invincible,	74	Jaxton.
Alfred,	74	Bayne.
Torbay,	74	Gidoin.

[1] Several of these names are incorrect. This should be J Williams In subsequent notes other errors are thus corrected

[2] Alan Gardner   [3] Sir Samuel Hood

Vessel.	Force.	Commanded by
Resolution,	74	Lt. Robert Manners.
Shrewsbury,	74	Knedget.
Canada,	74	Earl Cornwallis.[1]
Montagu,	74	Reduclas.[2]
Alcide,	74	C. Thompson.
Russell,	74	Saumarez.
Robust,	74	Crosby.
Valiant,	74	Baredney.[3]
Intrépide,	64	Molly.
Repulse,	64	Dumaresq.
Royal Oak,	74	Ademval.[4]
Belliqueux,	64	Camton.[5]
St. Alban's,	64	Inglis.
Prince William,	64	Wilkinson.
Prudent,	64	Barclay.
America,	64	S. Thompson.[6]

They had, moreover, 15[7] frigates, and had detached six vessels; 2698 pieces of cannon, besides those of the frigates

---

[1] Hon. William Cornwallis

[2] Bowen

[3] Goodall

[4] Burnet commanded this vessel. What name was meant in the text I do not know

[5] Sutherland commanded the *Belliqueux*

[6] The English list has also the *Monarch*, 74, Reynolds; the *Agamemnon*, 64, Caldwell, and *Magnificent*, 74, Linsee, but not the *Invincible*, *Robust* and *Intrépide*

[7] English accounts say 14

STATE OF THE FRENCH FLEET IN THE ENGAGEMENTS OF APRIL 9 AND 12, 1782.

VAN GUARD.

Vessel	Size	Captain
Pluto,	74	D'Albert de Rions.
Marseillais,	74	Castellane [1]
Conquérant,	74	La Grandière.[2]
Caton,	64	de Framont.
Bourgogne,	74	Charite [3]
Triomphant,	80	Count de Vaudreuil.
Magnifique,	74	de Macarty.[4]
Réflechy,	64	de Médine.[5]
Magnanime,	74	Le Bégue.[6]

[1] De Castellane Majastre was made commodore Nov 1, 1786

[2] Charles Marie, Count de la Grandière, was born at Brest in 1729 After 43 years service, 28 at sea, he was made commodore, Aug 20, 1784 He had then been present in eleven naval engagements He became rear admiral in 1792, and died at Rennes in 1812 His grandson, captain of a man of war, recently commanded the French division off the coast of Syria —*Biographie Bretonne, Etat de la France de Varoquier*

[3] De Charitte was made commodore Nov 1, 1786, and commanded the ninth squadron in 1789, rear-admiral in 1792

[4] Macteigue de Macarty, a brother of the celebrated Jesuit preacher, one of the ornaments of the modern French pulpit, was born in Dublin in 1769, son of Count Justin MacCarthy and Mary Winifred Tuite After the defeat of de Grasse, he sailed with Vaudreuil to Boston, where his vessel was lost on Lovel's Island He was then appointed to the America, a vessel presented by congress In 1789 he was major-general of the marine and of the squadrons at Rochefort

[5] De Médine was chief of division at Brest in 1789

[6] Le Bégue was made commodore in 1786

Vessel.	Size	Captain
Duc de Bourgogne,	80	Desphinousse.
Destin,	74	de Goimpy.
Diadême,	74	de Monteclerc.

CENTRAL DIVISION.

Vessel	Size	Captain
Glorieux,	74	*Desmars.*
Sceptre,	74	Marquis de Vaudreuil.
L'Eveillé,	64	de Tilly.[1]
Couronne,	80	Mithon.[2]
Ville de Paris,	104	Count de Grasse, admiral.
Languedoc,	80	Darous[2]
Dauphin Royal,	70	Monpéron
César,	74	De Marigny
Hector,	74	La Vicomté

REAR GUARD

Vessel	Size	Captain
Jason,	64	de Vilages[3]
Citoyen,	74	Déty

[1] Chevalier Le Gardeur de Tilly was apparently a Canadian of the Tilly branch of the family of Le Gardeur. The M. de St. Pierre, whom Washington met on the Ohio in 1753, was of the other branch, the Le Gardeur de Repentigny. Le Gardeur de Tilly had, in 1781, pursued Arnold in the *Chesapeake*, taken the *Romulus*, 44, and several transports. In 1789 he was commandant of the eighth squadron, at Rochefort, and commodore.

[2] De Mithon de Penouilly, and the Baron d'Arros d'Argelos, reached the grade of commodore Aug. 20, 1784.

[3] In 1789 de Villages was a commodore. He also commanded the seventh squadron.

UNDER THE COUNT DE GRASSE.

Brave,	74	d'Amblimont.[1]
Scipion,	74	de Clavel.[2]
Ardent,	66	de Gouzillon.
Zélé,	74	de Préville.
Auguste,	80	de Bougainville.
Northumberland,	74	de St. Césaire.
Palmier,	74	de Martilly.
Souverain,	74	de Glandvese.[3]
Neptune,	74	Dalins
Hercule,	74	*La Clochetcrie.*[4]

We had also six frigates; the *St. Esprit*, of 80 guns, was not with us, and on the 12th we had not the *Zélé*, *Caton*, nor *Jason*; 1974 cannon, without the frigates, in the affair of the 9th, and only 1772 in that of April 12.

On the 9th we had 724 guns less than the English, and on the 12th, 926. In the first engagement there were 4672 pieces of artillery in use, and in that of the 12th only 4470.

---

[1] Fuschemberg, Count d'Amblimont, General de Marine, was a commodore in 1784, but on the breaking out of the French revolution, entered the Spanish service, and was killed in February, 1797, in the battle gained by Lord St. Vincent

[2] The Chevalier Clavel was on the retired list in 1789

[3] De Glandvese was rear admiral in 1792

[4] The vessels in *italics* were taken in the action of April 12th, or just after it, and the captains in *italics* killed.

Chaudeau de la Clocheterie, killed in this last action of the war, was a highly distinguished officer, and opened the war in the Belle Poule by his brilliant action with the *Arethusa*, Marshall, in the face of an English fleet. He commanded the *Jason*, 64, in the fleet of De Ternay, which brought out Rochambeau, and in the skirmish with Commodore Cornwallis would have taken the *Ruby*, but for De Ternay's excessive prudence.

April 8. On the 8th of April, at 7, the convoy was under sail, escorted by the *Sagittaire* and *Experiment*. At 10 the fleet was also under way; two English vessels and a frigate were watching us as we started.[1] Rodney had, the same day, sent out a convoy, escorted by six vessels of the line and two frigates. As we made show of giving chase to the reconnoitering vessels they returned to St. Lucia, where they announced our movements. As soon as the fleet was out we took the starboard tack, the convoy keeping ahead and hugging the wind as much as possible. During the night we perceived the enemy's fleet.

6th combat, April 9. On the 9th, at early dawn, the rear frigate signalled sails, which proved to be the English fleet. We were then under Dominica, confounded with our convoy and becalmed. Our van, however, being at the mouth of the channel, to windward of the enemy, and we all having got in order, Mr. de Grasse made a signal for close action, while M. de Vaudreuil bore down directly on the first vessel of the English line, which had already begun to fire on the convoy, and forced it to hold up and even to bear away. Thus far the enemy's fleet was in good order; the French van had now rallied around their commo-

---

[1] One of these was the *Andromache*, Capt Byron, an active, brisk and intelligent officer.—LORD RODNEY, April 14, 1782

dore, when we tacked and were consequently ranged in the opposite order, steering with difficulty, but we soon after regained the weather-gage off Dominica channel; then our van, which had become our rear guard, attacked the English, who were becalmed except their van, now also a rear guard. We took the same tack (starboard) that they did. M. de Vaudreuil signalled to bear down on the enemy, which his squadron did. (M. de Grasse had placed in the squadron all the captains who had not displeased during the cruise, or those who he knew preferred their duty to their resentment.) The action began at 10,[1] and the fire began at rifle distance. This affair, of which there has been no detail in France, could not have been more hotly contested than it was for three hours and a half, between the two vans. The English van suffered extremely, for six of their vessels lost their top-gallants and two their main topmasts.[2] Very few vessels of the other divisions, either French or English, took part in this action, firing a little indeed, but too far off. The *Caton* having had the misfortune to have a cannon burst on board, which put eighty men *hors de combat*. We lost in this affair five officers and 120 men. The English lost

---

[1] 9 h. 30′

[2] The *Royal Oak* and *Montagu* were disabled, and the *Alfred* lost her captain, Bayne. *History of the War in America*, III, 354

rather more than we did.[1] The *Auguste* and the *Zélé* were in the rear of our fleet, which served as an excuse for M. de Grasse, who should have brought the English to a general engagement, for he had the weather-gage, with a fresh wind, which they had not. Should he not have attacked their van with all his forces? Surely fourteen vessels could not have stood the fire of thirty-four; and this division of their fleet would have been destroyed before it could have been relieved by the other division of the fleet, which was in a dead calm; then fall on the detached vessels of the centre one after the other, and he would have had them at his own terms, as Mr. Rodney showed him three days after.[2]

A man must be unfortunate enough, it must be admitted, to let such fine occasions slip; but, though our admiral might entertain fears for the two rear vessels, the English were becalmed, and we would have so cut up their van, and even their center, as to deprive them of all idea of picking up our laggards, who had Dominica and Martinique to put in to. Nothing in my opinion can excuse Admiral de Grasse in this affair, from which he might have derived the greatest honor. During the action the convoy was anchored at Guadaloupe, where it was certainly secure. It

---

[1] For Rodney's account of this action, see *Appendix*

[2] For a defence of de Grasse's conduct on this occasion see the following journal

UNDER THE COUNT DE GRASSE.

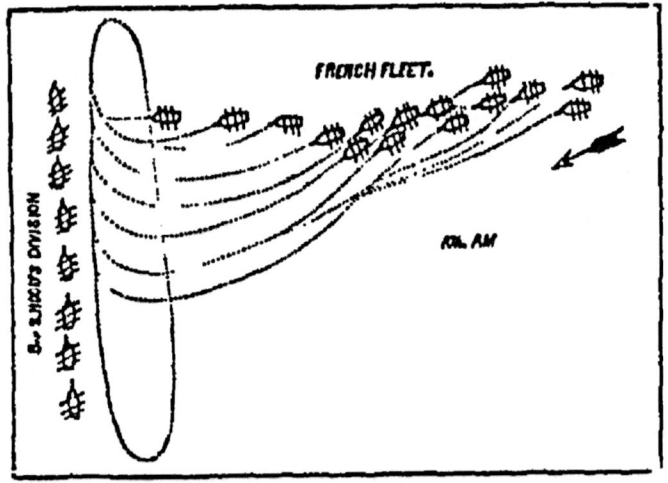

Action of April 9th.

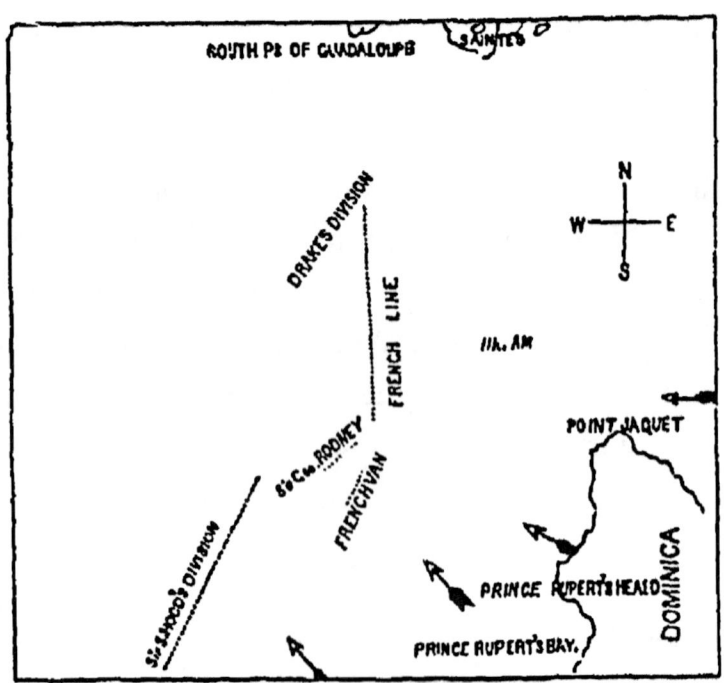

Action of April 12th

seems that for the four last months that M. de Grasse commanded, his only care was to commit the greatest blunders. The only advantage we derived from this affair was, that the field of battle was left to us; a very trifling advantage at sea. The preservation of our convoy is indeed one. It sailed next day from Guadaloupe for Cap François, and it had the good fortune not to be molested on its route. The *Caton* also left us in the evening and anchored at the Basse Terre of Guadaloupe, after receiving the admiral's orders.

On the 10th we lost sight of the English, and we hugged the wind so as to double the channel of Saintes.

On the 11th we were engaged in the same manœuvre. The *Zélé* ran foul of the *Jason* and rendered her unable to keep the sea. She then ran into several others. I believe, indeed, that all on board of her had lost their senses. She at last ran into the *Ville de Paris*, and in this collision lost her bowsprit and foremast. A frigate had to take her in tow for the Basse Terre at Guadaloupe, and then it was an incredible time before she ran her cables through the hawse holes. It is impossible to behave worse than this vessel did from the 8th till the morning of the 12th. She brought on the hottest, longest and most terrible, and I may say the most dishonorable sea-fight since the invention of gunpowder.

7th combat, April 12. On the 12th, at daybreak, the king's fleet being under Marie Galante, we perceived the *Zélé* dismasted three leagues to our leeward, and the *Ville de Paris* at one league. At the same time we discovered the English van trying to close with the *Zélé*.[1] Mr. de Grasse then made the signal to clear for action and form in line in inverse order. As may be supposed, from our trying to double a channel, we were in the greatest disorder. The signal was executed by crowding sail and by taking the opposite tack from the English fleet. Then it was that Mr. de Pavillon,[2] an officer of the greatest merit, foreseeing the result, and the blunder about to be committed if these signals were made, twice sent the adjutant of the *Triomphant* to distinguish the colors of the flags; and when he confirmed the fact that they really prescribed the manœuvres in question, that excellent officer, losing his temper, went aloft himself, tried two glasses, and exclaimed: "Wretched day!" Then turning to Mr. de Vaudreuil he said: "General, you are going to see a terrible affair, which will be most disastrous to France." The French fleet kept form-

---

[1] The ensuing account throws less blame on the *Zélé*, of whose commander, de Préville, I find no further note.

[2] John Francis du Cheyron du Pavillon, born at Périgueux Sept. 29, 1730, entered the army at fifteen as sub-lieutenant, but at eighteen entered the navy, and soon became the superintendent of instruction of the younger officers. He wrote a work on naval tactics, published in 1778; introduced a system of signals by day and night. He commanded several vessels with distinction, and fell on the fatal 12th of April, 1782.

ing, necessarily to the windward of the enemy's line. At 7.50 the fire began, and soon after we were becalmed under Dominica; an event that M. de Grasse should have foreseen, as there is rarely any wind under the isles, which are extremely elevated. From the state of the fleets as given above, it will be seen that the English had 926 pieces of cannon over us when we engaged in the most disastrous of sea fights. We ran along the English line till the moment when the *Glorieux* was run into by Lord Rodney's forward second, a three-decker of ninety guns, which threw her three masts overboard and swept her clean as a pontoon. This was the first place where our line was broken,[1] for the calm that held us gave them great advantage, and enabled them to break through our line in three places; and they threw it into a confusion that M. de Grasse made no attempt to remedy.[2] The

---

[1] This explains how Rodney was able to effect the operation which brought him so much glory As soon as he saw the breach he kept a close luff and passed through All now admit that the manœuvre was not deliberately planned, although the advocates of Rodney so claimed

[2] The late Commander Ward, in his masterly work on naval tactics, discussing this action, says that the only advantage that this movement gave the English was that it attacked the unprepared side of the French rear, and that if De Grasse with his rear following had luffed to leeward of the English rear, engaging it closely and continuously with his post batteries, Rodney's manœuvre would have been fruitless Instead of hugging to his enemy however, De Grasse most unwisely and ruinously bore up, and endeavored to escape on a line at right angles to his former line On which, the English rear steered off on a parallel course before the wind, and the English van wore round, thus taking the French rear between two fires, making defeat absolutely annihilating, when, had he fought it out instead of trying to escape, he would in all probability have avoided any considerable injury.

English admiral, on the other hand, restored order in his fleet, and had always fifteen or twenty vessels in line. The *Glorieux* having been dismasted, fell to leeward, and was at the same time surrounded by the enemy. Our admiral, followed by two or three vessels, went to its relief and tried to save it, but all in vain. In this sad plight it received a terrible renewal of fire, which it answered so violently that we thought they had set it on fire, using all their guns. It retarded by this means the loss of the vessel, but unfortunately only for a moment. The frigate *Richemont* took her in tow and had drawn her off about half a league when the officer in command of the *Glorieux* seeing the enemy's bullets again pouring in, losing all hope of escape and not wishing the frigate sunk or taken, seeing too that she would not abandon him, himself cut the tow-line. In her dismasting, this vessel had lost her captain, the brave and untiring Baron Descars, many of her officers, and a great part of her crew.[1]

During this time we kept fighting on, sometimes with one vessel, sometimes with three, often with two. Occasionally the fire would hold up for fifteen minutes, but only to begin again more violently. The Marquis de Vaudreuil, always in the hottest of the fire, rallied his division as well as he could. At 2, the *César* finding herself to the windward of our fleet was surrounded by the enemy, and after a bloody action was forced to strike, having her cap-

---

[1] She was taken possession of by the *Royal Oak*.

tain, Mr. de Marigny, mortally wounded, and having lost a great many. M. de Grasse had lost his wits; made no more signals; sought every post of danger, followed by his two seconds, till the *Couronne* abandoned him at half past 3. The *Languedoc*, sheathed with wood and two years old at that, could not keep up with the copper-sheathed *Ville de Paris*, but it is a settled fact that the Baron d'Aross retired only with the Marquis de Vaudreuil. The *Hector*, finding herself in the midst of the enemy, sustained the most stubborn and terrible action possible. She looked like a blazing furnace vomiting fire and iron. After losing her captain, M. de la Vicomté, with six feet of water in her hold and incapable of further resistance, she struck.[1] At 6 the *Ardent* was taken, and fought shortly before surrendering.[2] M. de Grasse, still in the midst of the fire, having exhausted his ammunition, was forced to surrender,[3] although M. de Vaudreuil offered to take him in tow. That vessel had lost rigging, sails and rudder; her masts ready to go by the board. There was on board the *Ville de Paris* a quantity of money belonging to the merchants of the Windward Isles, and the army chest,

---

[1] She was engaged by the *Alcide* and *Canada* and struck to the former.

[2] Taken by the *Belliqueux*.

[3] The *Ville de Paris* was engaged by the *Canada* and *Russell*, when the *Barfleur* came up and poured in a broadside from the stern. Ross, in his life of Saumarez says that the *Russell*, Saumarez's vessel, engaged her first.

a circumstance which heightened the dishonor of seeing the admiral taken.

M. de Vaudreuil effected the retreat of the fleet with his squadron, which was in the centre of the angle of chase formed by the English, and which Rear Admiral Hood wished to close. We certainly could not have escaped had not Rodney twice opposed this manœuvre, saying that a bridge of gold must be left a flying foe. Before striking, M. de Grasse made the signal of *sauve qui peut*. The action ended at 7.32.

M. de Martelly, commanding the *Palmier*, had struck, but the English prize crew on the *Cesar* having got drunk and set her on fire,[1] he took it for the *Shrewsbury*. An auxiliary officer then asked his leave to save the ship. M. de Martelly, charmed with the proposal, told him that he had only to act as he pleased, and the officer in fact saved the vessel. The English having opened the angle of chase, left us at liberty to retire, which we did without noise or show of light.

M. Rodney[2] ordered astern Mr. Hood, who had twice wished to close the angle of chase. It was fortunate for us that that officer did not command, as he is deemed more able than the fortunate Rodney. We lost in this engagement 3500 men, killed or taken, and many officers of distinction. The English got off

---

[1] In the conflagration, the survivors of her crew (Allen says 400, *History of the Civil War*, III, 255, 200), with an English lieutenant and 60 seamen perished.

[2] Rodney's account of this his most famous achievement will be found in the appendix.

with 1800, and many officers, and their ships were worse cut up than ours.¹ We sustained an irreparable loss in the fall of Mr. de Pavillon, a unique man: the very English regretted him, acknowledging his talents. He was wounded early in the action, and died next day. He had his leg broken. He forgot his pain to inquire the position of the fleets, which were mingled together till some of ours were taken and others drew off the field of battle, when only the division of the Marquis de Vaudreuil remained in good order, not having lost a vessel nor been very severely handled, although the English stated in one of their reports that the *Diadème* was sunk.

I will not omit the gallant manœuvre made by two of our vessels, the *Destin* and the *Magnanime*, which followed each other. Seeing Rodney bear down with his two seconds, all three-deckers, and deeming it not a time to be at ease, the *Destin* bore up in the face of the *Duke*, poured in a broadside, not three bullets of which fell into the water; then, keeping the wind, cannonaded her on one side, while the *Magnanime* did as much, till bearing down in her turn, she swept the *Duke* from the stern, carrying her two galleries overboard. This vessel was kept engaged by the *Reflechy*, and *Diadème*, and struck to the *Triomphant*; but M. de Vaudreuil could not man her, having no boats nor time. She had lost her foremast, which the *Diadème*

¹ The English give their loss at 12 officers killed and wounded, 240 men killed, 797 wounded. Total, 1069, and the French at 3000.

shot away. Another English vessel also struck, but the same reasons prevented our taking it. At the close of the fight, the English had eleven vessels under the wind unable to molest us.[1] At night fall each made sail after his own fashion, executing admirably M. de Grasse's last signal.[2]

A circumstance that heightened still more the horror of that day, was the prodigious number of sharks that swarmed in the sea, and which devoured the men as soon as they reached the water (for as soon as a man is killed he is thrown overboard). There were certainly more than a thousand of these creatures following the vessels of the two fleets.

On the 13th we found five fugitives assembled, and the next day we fell in with Mr. de Vaudreuil. We were then seventeen: four vessels of our rear guard went to Curaçoa, a Dutch post, with Commodore Bougainville. M. de Framont, captain commanding

---

[1] It was a matter of consolation to the French that England had no trophies of this victory, for not a vessel taken that day reached England. The Cesar we have seen was burnt, and on their passage home the Ville de Paris, Hector and Glorieux all foundered. We, too, may feel our national pride relieved, in the fact that no English crowd ever flocked to see brought in as a prize the vessel on which Washington, de Grasse, and Rochambeau had met.

[2] The first news of this action in the United States, was an account in Rivington's Royal Gazette, taken from the Antigua Gazette, but it was naturally received with great doubt, the more especially as Captain Keane of the Hulker privateer, who had seen part of the action, contradicted the English account. A species of gambling at once commenced in the shape of policies on the French fleet, warm Whigs insuring largely at high rates, and when the news was confirmed some were ruined. Among these were Blair McClenachan

the *Caton*, imprudently left Guadaloupe with the *Jason*, and they were taken in the channel of Porto Rico by an English squadron of ten ships and a frigate.[1]

The tidings of our disaster having preceded us at the cape, the Spanish ships which lay there, ten in number, came out to cover the entrance of the king's fleet. I know nothing more humiliating than this.

We anchored accordingly on the 26th, and found already there the *Couronne, Brave, Duc de Bourgogne* and *Magnifique*. These vessels were not in good odor in the fleet, especially the first two.

Our stay at the cape was spent in refitting, repairs worse made than at Martinique, this colony being actually destitute of everything. We formed however sorts of shops to put all in order as soon as possible, and the naval officers connected with the port had their hands full at that time. M. de Montéclerc superintended these works, and it was certainly no fault of his that everything was not put in good condition at the least possible expense, and M. de Vaudreuil could not have made a better choice. The patriotism and ability of this old and excellent officer, had been long known in France; the department in which he was, alone in its jealousy refused its praise, till compelled to bestow it, and for once it was just. But after recognizing his zeal and talents, they should

---

[1] The *Caton* and *Jason*, with the frigate *Aimable* and corvette *Ceres* were captured by Sir Samuel Hood in the *Barfleur*, with the *Valiant* and *Magnificent*.

have aspired to imitate him. M. de Bougainville and the four vessels which went to Curaçoa arrived at the cape a week after us; the *Auguste* had been roughly handled, having had 80 men killed on board; and the *Hercule* having lost her captain M. de la Clocheterie. They brought back from that emporium, cordage which we greatly needed, the rigging of the fleet being cut up.

May

M. de Montéclerc effected the repairs so promptly that on the 30th of May we sent out a convoy escorted by the *Saint Esprit*, which had arrived from Martinique a week before, after being chased by several English vessels. The *Destin*, the *Conquerant* and the *Réfléchy* were under her orders. The *Sceptre*[1] left us next day to go and destroy an English trading post at Hudson's Bay, with two frigates and detachments of infantry. The regiment of Armagnac furnished most.

---

[1] The celebrated La Pérouse commanded this expedition, and met with all success. It is somewhat strange that De Goussencourt does not name him. Jean François Galaup de La Pérouse was born at Alby in 1741, was educated at the navy school; became a midshipman November 19, 1756, and in his fifth cruise was wounded and taken prisoner in the *Formidable*, Du Verger, at the battle of Bellisle. Ensign October 1, 1764, he became commander of the *Adour* in 1767. In 1779 he commanded the *Amazone*, in d'Estaing's fleet, in the engagement with Byron, then took the *Ariel*, off New England. Appointed captain April 4, 1780, in the *Astrea*, and with La Touche took the *Charlestown* and *Jack*. After which he sailed to Cape François where he was appointed to the *Sceptre*. In the expedition here referred to he commanded the *Sceptre*, having under him the frigates *Astrée*, De Langle, and *Engageant*, La Jaille, with 200 infantry and artillery under Major de Rostaing, 4 field pieces, 2 mortars and 300 bombs

Three or four days after there sailed for the Windward Isles the *Dauphin Royal*, the *Sagittaire* and the *Experiment*, with a part of the troops taken from these garrisons. I had forgotten to state that General, the Marquis de Bouillé, had arrived at the cape shortly after us, and knew our disaster. He had a long conference with the Marquis de Vaudreuil, Señor Galvez and Señor Solano and two or three other general officers, the result of which was that nothing should be undertaken; and the next day the ten thousand Spaniards who had arrived at the cape in Solano's squadron, were distributed in the island. This infantry was superb and very well kept, but a little dirty.

June On the 16th six of our vessels left the cape and went down the coast to collect the vessels of the convoy preparing for France, under the escort of the *Languedoc*, *Diadème*, *Marsellais* and *Magnanime*.

After struggling through the ice, he reached Fort Prince of Wales on the 8th of August, and soon reduced that fort and Forts York and Nelson. His conquest showed the generosity usual to the French He left supplies for the English in the interior, and exacted the publication of Hearne's voyage, of which he found the manuscript there In 1785 he sailed from Brest, in the *Boussole* and *Astrolabe*, to make a voyage around the world, and after exploring the Pacific from Behring's straits to Botany bay, sent home in 1788 an account of his voyage No tidings of him reaching France, the National Convention in 1791 sent out an expedition in search of him, but it returned without effecting anything; and it was not till 1825–8 that Dillon and d'Urville established the fact that he perished on Vanikoro During his absence La Pérouse was made commodore, November 2d, 1786 His voyage was published in Paris in 4 vols 4to, in 1797, and in English at London in 1799.

They were also directed to take in powder at St. Nicholas mole, as there was very little in the fleet. Under Tortugas they handed over the convoy to the escorting vessels, and returned to the anchorage at the cape. It was somewhat surprising to see two convoys set out unopposed by the English. Having returned to France with this convoy, I will give an account of this voyage; but I shall first give some account of the manners, customs, and religious state of this country in 1782.

Most of the French who go to the West Indies count on getting rich very fast, and returning home as soon as possible. They exhaust the land by over-cultivation, and take none of the comforts of life; differing greatly in this from the English. They keep *economes*, a kind of superintendents, who ruin them, and end by becoming masters of the plantations which they direct. The creole thinks only of his pleasures; gaming, love, and the table, take up all his moments. A part of the night is spent in very high play. I have seen few countries where gambling prevails as much as at Martinique, and not one that comes up to the cape, and the manner of playing there. Love is his dominant passion, although the easiest satisfied. The climate and food contribute, doubtless, as much as the facility of obtaining women. The slaves, and even all the colored girls, prize nothing so much as the embrace of a white; and as they are very agreeable, they are preferred to white women, who, on the other hand, have to stoop to vile arts to gratify their inclination, and they never keep a lover sighing three whole days. A fine table, the most exquisite viands, cost the easy creole nothing; and of all men, they seem most to enjoy things with gusto. I can say that there is no sense that they do not gratify in the course of the day. From this sketch it may be inferred that it is surprising to see a creole grow old. Many have died of dissipation, and they die every day. This is the reason why so few young men return from the West Indies. Religion is known only by name in this country; good faith being absolutely banished, and virtue scarcely practiced by those whose employment or office is intended to make it respected and enforced. This country is absolutely corrupted. The children go naked, and run about the streets and squares, where they commit great indecencies. If nature has given the inhabitants of the torrid zone means to exhaust every possible kind of pleasure, it has placed the chastisement at hand, for how many diseases afflict this wretched country! There are few in France to be compared, in violence, to those of Southern America. I shall not enter into any details as to them, it would be too long and too revolting. I leave this to the Esculapiuses. The productions, animals, birds, fish, are not in my line, and are too well known for me to dwell on them.

July   On the first of July we set sail, favored by the wind. We got most happily out of the Mogane channel.

On the 9th of July we were off Bermuda, which we had infinite trouble to pass, the winds having become contrary. Our voyage was chequered by all sorts of weather, mostly contrary to us. A hundred leagues north and south of the Banks of Newfoundland, we fell in with an English cartel going to Boston, which we examined strictly. About this latitude we saw a very extraordinary fish, which Mr. Buffon does not know of. This animal is about sixty feet long, of the form of a ray, with an elevation three feet high on the back-bone, to which a white shark-shaped fish was attached. We could not take it, although it was along side of us, for half an hour.

At the altitude of the Azores we fell in with a Portuguese man of war, which must have taken us for English, as we all had the flag of that nation hoisted.

August. August 13th, estimating ourselves fifty leagues from Isle de Groas, and our convoy sailing very badly, we sailed but a short distance, especially as we had no frigate to explore our route.

The night of the 17–18th we had a heavy gale of wind, the more dangerous as we were near land. Most of us, I assure you, gave ourselves up as lost, and never expected to see day or reach France. Our masts strained, yet we had to carry sail or perish. Had we been dismasted, we should undoubtedly have swamped. It is easy to imagine how we spent the night. At last, after being well buffeted, we perceived the island called Belleisle, where we anchored all but three ships, which made L'orient.

The next morning several of us went ashore. It is impossible to convey the pleasure we all felt in treading upon the soil of France. Some kissed it, others lay down on it; there was no childishness that we did not do. The *Marseillais* having been commissioned to convey the merchantmen over the river at Bordeaux, remained another day at this anchorage. As for us, we sailed on the 21st, three men of war, and a small vessel for Brest.

On the 22d we discovered four vessels which we at first took to be English, which did not please us over much. At last, after much trouble, we passed the *Bec du Raz*, the *Bay des Trepassés*, saw the fort of Port Ric, and at last, on the 23d of August, arrived at the roadstead of Brest. Few days have appeared so interesting to the author of this journal, by name,

le Chev. de Goussincourt.

END OF THE JOURNAL

ERRATA

Mr du Plessis Pascault commanded the *Intrépide* at the time of her loss by fire.

The Count de Vaudreuil commanded the *Sceptre*, and the Marquis, his brother, in the *Triomphant*, commanded the French fleet after our defeat on the 12th of April, and the capture of Mr. de Grasse

JOURNAL
OF AN OFFICER
IN THE
NAVAL ARMY IN AMERICA,
IN 1781 AND 1782

Magnus sæclorum nascitur ordo — *Virgil*

AMSTERDAM, 1783.

JOURNAL.

The thirteen United States of North America had declared themselves sovereign and independent in 1776. So far were they from being so in 1781, that those in the south were on the point of being compelled to acknowledge their former master, which would have rendered the liberty of the others very uncertain Nevertheless, England, at the close of 1782, declared them all free.

The relation of these successes forms part of the campaign of the Count de Grasse. In this view it is offered entire to the public, as the check which the arms of France sustained on the 12th of April, 1782, did not embolden England to continue her non-recognition of the sovereignty of the United States; the advantages obtained in 1781, must, therefore, have established it beyond peradventure.

The events of 1780, and of the first months of 1781, had not even prepared those of the rest of that year and of the early months of the next. In 1780, the fleet of the two powers had fought no less than three times, without obtaining any decisive advantage. The empire of the West India waters remained unsettled, and no enterprise was undertaken on either side before wintering. When that time arrived there were but four French ships at Martinique, and five at St. Domingo; the rest escorting a very numerous convoy, did not enter Brest till January 4, 1781, after a voyage of five months.

On the 16th of March following, there was an engagement in Delaware river between the French squadron which had wintered at Newport, and the English fleet stationed at New York.[1] This action was very spirited and well maintained on both sides; but the debarkation of the French and American troops on one of the banks of that river, which the English sought to prevent, was not in fact effected; hence, without being able to claim the victory, they reaped the advantages of one. Charleston and Carolina had returned to the power of England in 1780, and an English army ravaged Virginia in 1781, while a flotilla of that nation wasted with fire and sword both shores of Chesapeake Bay.

'Such was the situation of the belligerent parties in America, when the Count de Grasse was appointed to command the king's naval forces in that part of the world. He was not known to the new minister of the

---

[1] This was the action between the French fleet under the Chevalier Destouches, and the English fleet under Arbuthnot and Graves The object was to take Arnold at Portsmouth, and it did not, of course, take place in Delaware river, but off Cape Henry Soulé's *History des Troubles*, iii, 364. *History of the Civil War*, iii, 180

navy. He had been obliged, in consequence of his health (having been in constant service since 1775), to refuse the command of the squadrons which had remained in 1780 at Martinique and St. Domingo. Hence he did not expect and could not expect to return thither so soon, still less to be commander-in-chief there. He represented the state of his health, the necessity of his enjoying his native air, and that, moreover, as the departure of the fleet could not take place soon enough to carry out any operation before wintering, he would infallibly be reproached with this inactivity; he even went so far as to name an officer, whom he deemed more capable than himself to fill the post; but the king insisted on being obeyed, and at once. On this the Count de Grasse, who had reached Paris, February 1st, left the 18th, and arrived at Brest on the 26th.

There a considerable squadron was preparing, which was to escort a convoy of one hundred and fifty sail, with a reinforcement of troops; but, as some of the vessels were part of the squadron which had returned from Cadiz on the 4th of January, it required time to put them in condition to make a new campaign. In spite of his infirmities, the Count de Grasse, by his presence in the arsenal from five in the morning, hastened the fitting out, but the arrival at Brest of the new minister of the navy expedited it still more, and the fleet and convoy set sail, March 22d, with a favorable wind, in spite of the equinox.

We doubled the cape on the 27th; and then, to keep the convoy always together, and to prevent the sailing of the slow craft from retarding that of the rest, the admiral had them towed by his ships, taking one himself.

Thanks to this precaution, in thirty-six days the fleet and the whole convoy (an unheard of thing till then for so many vessels), came at day-break, on the 28th of April, in sight of the land of Martinique.

The cutter *Alerte* had announced their arrival; they passed through the channel of St. Lucia, so as to reach their destination three days sooner, and to avoid a calm, if they met the English squadron, supposed to be at sea.

In fact, at 11, an English frigate was perceived making signals, and at 2 o'clock twenty-two hostile sails were signalled towards *Diamond Rock*. The convoy could not have entered the roadstead of Martinique, except by night, and it would have been imprudent to try it, in the presence of so large a hostile squadron, because there was no way of knowing whether vessels had not been left at St. Lucia, which might rout the convoy while the two squadrons were engaged. Accordingly, the French fleet passed the night near the shore and athwart Point Salines, awaiting the intelligence which the general sent for by an officer whom he put ashore at Point St. Anne. This officer returned to the fleet at 8 p. m., and reported that 17 vessels of the line and five frigates had, for the last fifty days, blockaded the roadstead of Fort Royal and the four French vessels anchored there: the latter had orders, during the course of the night, to hoist sail the next morning and attack the head or rear of the English squadron, as soon as they saw the French fleet.

On the 29th, in the morning, the fleet, covering the convoy, steered for Fort Royal; at 8 o'clock the English squadron was signalled, and at noon the French fleet was on the beam of the English flagship. The English began a very distant fire, to which the French paid no attention till the English bullets went far beyond them. The convoy had lain to the windward of Diamond Rock,[1] and when the action began it continued its route to its destination, without the loss of a single vessel from its leaving Brest.

The English fleet, while fighting, crowded sail; the admiral sent orders by the frigates for each French vessel to engage the English vessel opposite, and for the surplus with the four vessels from the roadstead of Fort Royal, as a light squadron to turn the English line and get it between two fires. This order was not executed. Of the English fleet only three vessels of the rear guard were ever engaged, because the French van which served as rear guard, instead of bearing down, according to all the signals, kept the wind constantly with light sails, while, on the contrary, the rear guard became van, bore down on the enemy and

---

[1] A rock at the entrance of Fort Royal Bay

engaged them vigorously. Thus the English fleet could always bear away in order; and at six o'clock there were only thirteen out of the twenty-four French vessels in pursuit of the seventeen English; these covered the retreat of the *Russell*, 74, which then ran before the wind to St. Eustatius, where it arrived with seven feet of water in the hold, and much cut up; the *Centaur*, the *Torbay*, the *Intrépide*, were not less so.

The admiral sent most precise orders to all his fleet to keep together during the night, so as to renew the action in the morning; but on the 30th, at daybreak, although the head of the French fleet was within cannon shot and a half of the English flagship, the French fleet had not rallied, as it might and should have been, as the *Souverain* (the Chevalier de Glandevese, captain), second of the commander of the rear guard, manœuvred so well, that in the morning she found herself second to the admiral, who then directed the part of the fleet that was with him, so as to make the English take a route to facilitate the rest of the French in overtaking them; but they had not got together by evening.

The night of April 30, May 1, was spent in chasing the enemy under all sail; the English, on their side, made all sail, wind astern. On the morning of May 1st there were only eleven French vessels near enough to attack the enemy; the others were excessively behind, and some out of sight. It would have been imprudent to begin a new action with eleven ships against sixteen of so superior sailing qualities, and without any hope of being reinforced during the action by the rest of the fleet. Had the pursuit of the enemy been continued, it would clearly have been useless, and time, which was precious, would have been wasted in regaining the wind; for the fleet was already thirty leagues west of St. Lucia. The chase was accordingly discontinued at 10 o'clock, and we were all in the sulks; for since the 29th none of us would have missed his share in the prizes and glory.

The French fleet resumed its route, and anchored, May 6th, at Martinique, where, since the commencement of the war, the Marquis de Bouillé, the honor of his nation in this part of the world, commanded.

The naval and military commanders lost no time in their operations; it seems that they wished to undertake nothing the execution of which was not certain, before the 1st of July, since they decided to attack the isle of Tobago, the only one that interrupted the communication of the French Windward Isles with the Spanish mainland. This communication, established from isle to isle, secured fresh provisions, not abundant on the islands, and deprived the hostile cruisers of all refuge in those ports.

The Marquis de Bouillé had also a project of forming an establishment at Gros Islet, on St. Lucia, as there was not time enough to attempt a regular attack on the Morne Fortuné; he proposed to fortify Gros Islet in six weeks. The isle of St. Lucia would then become half English and half French; the enemy would be deprived of the best anchorage in the island, and that most annoying to Martinique; but prudence required that force enough should be landed to keep the garrison of Morne Fortuné in check, examine on the spot the extent and situation of the works to be raised, and the time necessary to perfect them.

These two plans would be carried out at the same time, by letting the fleet cruise to the windward of St. Lucia, after it had protected the landing of the Marquis de Bouillé. The fleet in this position being to windward of the enemy's, would have been able to oppose any attack on his part.

In consequence, on the 8th of May a vessel of 64 guns (M. d'Albert de Rions, captain of a ship of the line), and two of fifty, were sent, with transports loaded with troops and ammunition, under the order of M. de Blanchelande,[1] to revictual the isles of St. Vincent and Granada, and then to attack Tobago.[2]

---

[1] Philibert Frances Rouxel de Blanchelande, born at Dijon in 1735, was the son of a lieutenant colonel, who died of his wounds in 1740. He entered the service at the age of 12, and in 1779 came to America as major of the regiment of Auxerrois. He soon became lieutenant colonel, and after his successful defence of St Vincent was made brigadier, and in 1781 governor of Tobago, and next of Dominica. Having retired to private life in France, Louis XVI made him governor of St Domingo; but after the revolution began he was superseded, tried by a revolutionary tribunal in France, and condemned to death, April 11, 1793. His son soon followed him to the guillotine.   S

[2] This detachment was large enough for its object; it was deemed very rash in France, without considering that it was to operate to leeward

The fleet having set sail the same day, the Marquis de Bouillé landed with 1200 men at Gros Islet, Saint Lucia, and surprised a hundred men, who were guarding that post; after reconnoitering the ground in person, he saw that the time was too short to finish, before winter, retrenchments solid enough in case of attack; the troops reëmbarked with the prisoners; the fleet escorted them to Fort Royal, where it anchored May 15.[1]

The enemy were still at St. Christopher's; but on the 22d news came that they had sailed and were manœuvring to windward. The French fleet again set sail on the 25th, to go and cover the attack on Tobago. The French had landed there on the 24th, and the artillery of the vessels had soon silenced the batteries which defended the anchorage; the fleet came in sight of the island on the 30th; it perceived six hostile vessels with a convoy, destined, doubtless, to carry in supplies; but they renounced their project by a prompt flight. On the 31st the fleet landed the Marquis de Bouillé, with a corps of troops, at Courland Bay, and on the 1st of June, the Marquis du Chilleau, with other troops, at Man of War's Bay.

These reinforcements were necessary; Mr. de Blanchelande had driven the garrison of the island into a very strong post, whence the enemy could retire

---

[1] This should apparently be the 18th See preceding journal S

from morno to morno, and hold out till winter. The Marquis de Bouillé and M. du Chilleau advanced each on his side to the rear of the post: three different attacks were concerted for the 2d of June; but the Marquis de Bouillé having summoned the enemy to surrender, they saw themselves so surrounded and hopeless of relief, that they accepted the terms granted to the island of Dominica.

The day of June 3 was spent in reëmbarking the troops, with the prisoners, after leaving all that was needed for the subsistence and defence of that island.

On the 4th, the frigates, which were cruising to windward, announced the approach of the enemy's fleet and a convoy.

On the 5th, the English, to the number of twenty-one ships of the line, and 17 others of inferior size, seemed disposed to fight. The French, who had hoisted sail the night before, formed in line to meet them; but the English soon bore away: they did not even wait for the French to be at the same distance from them as the six vessels which had sheered off on the 30th of May. The army having all reëmbarked, the fleet resumed its station to the windward.

It sailed on the 10th for Granada, where it anchored June 11th, it left there the 14th, and anchored on the 19th at Fort Royal, Martinique, bringing in all the prizes made in the cruise and at the conquered island.

Winter had been proclaimed already at Martinique, by the overflow of the rivers; but it was necessary to lay in the provisions, water and wood of the whole fleet, and repair some vessels which greatly needed it. The fleet could not leave Fort Royal before July 5th; it took its way to St. Domingo, where it arrived on the 16th, with a convoy of 150 merchantmen.

Half an hour after midnight, on that day, the *Ville de Paris* struck three times, but without stopping, on a bank of rock or sand unknown to all the charts; she was then three leagues N. N. W. of LaGrange,[1] and running four knots, under bare poles.

The fleet had been increased to 24 ships of the line, by the junction of the division which it found at Martinique, and to 29 by the five which were at the cape, returning from the expedition to Pensacola, under the orders of Chevalier de Monteil, commodore; four of these vessels had gone out to meet a convoy escorted by the frigate *Fée*, and they joined the fleet. Another, under the command of the Chevalier de Glandeve, captain of a ship, had orders to pass south of the island, to take under escort all the trading vessels that wished to profit by it. As it was discovered that there were two hostile frigates which might intercept the *Fée* (M. de Boubée, captain), two vessels were detached to chase them. They did it successfully, for that frigate, which, having already sustained two actions, that had wounded its masts, had just fought a third under Tortugas.

[1] It would be well to examine this shoal for the safety of navigation

On the 25th of July, at half past six, A. M., an accident befell the *Intrépide*, 74, which might have destroyed the whole fleet at the anchorage. The vessel took fire, and the flames were instantly so violent that it was impossible to extinguish them. The vessel was drawn from amid the fleet and run ashore; everything with oars was most zealously employed to save the crew, and the vessel blew up a few minutes after.[1]

A similar accident, almost at the same time, befell from the same cause, the frigate *Constante*, near Isle à Vache. She formed part of a detachment of the fleet sent south of St. Domingo: she ran on shoals; the boats could not get near enough to save all the crew; only a midshipman and 175 men were saved.

On arriving at the cape, the admiral found the frigate *Concorde*, from North America. The news spread that the dispatches of the naval and military commanders, and those of the envoy of France, at Philadelphia, joined in assuring him that, without a prompt relief of vessels, men, money and ammunition, Virginia would fall again under the English yoke; and that the French army had pay only to the 20th of August. These fears and these wants were set forth without fixed projects to remedy them; they left the admiral a choice only between an attack on New York by sea and by land, or to transfer the theatre of war to Virginia by a sudden occupation of Chesapeake

---

[1] A barrel of taffia, which took fire from the candle of the dealer out, caused this terrible conflagration.

Bay with sufficient naval forces. For either plan, nothing less was asked than a reinforcement of 6000 men, 1,200,000 livres in specie, munitions in proportion, and all in the course of August; without all this relief, the most disastrous events were menaced. The admiral's reply was expected by the same frigate.[1]

The movement of the combined armies on New York had been announced; a movement necessary for the first plan, and facilitating the execution of the second.

The admiral was not unaware that the English West India fleet was about to sail for the most part to North America, that a squadron from Europe, under Admiral Digby, was on its way to the same point; that Lord Cornwallis was, with his army in Virginia, destroying warehouses, shipyards, ships, carrying off negroes and cattle. The American troops might, indeed, harass him in his march; but deprived all naval protection, they durst not approach the shores of the Chesapeake, for fear of being cut off. The attack on New York would certainly have delivered Virginia; but its success was more doubtful than the defeat of Lord Cornwallis, in Virginia itself. To ensure the success of this, required only the sudden occupation of Chesapeake Bay with a commanding fleet. The French commander soon resolved to transport his whole force there; but it was necessary to provide

---

[1] This agrees mainly with the statement in Rochambeau's *Memoirs*, ii, 277 s

for the security of the coasts and commerce of St. Domingo during his absence; it required a considerable amount of specie, a powerful reinforcement of troops, munitions of all kinds, and to be at the Chesapeake by the month of August. He had not near the aid required in men and money; eighteen hundred men had been left sick at Martinique, and he must expect to leave as many more at St. Domingo; the admiral had instructions from the court only as to some escorts and cruises. I know not whether he was sure enough of its confidence in him to hope that his project, useful and glorious as it might be to the French navy, would not be reproached by all in case of failure; he had to create all the means, and had only twenty days to provide for everything.[1] There happened to be at St. Domingo a commissary from the island of Cuba; it was agreed with him that a Spanish squadron should protect the coasts and commerce; and as about three thousand four hundred men could be spared from St. Domingo, till the month of

---

[1] The publicity recently given by order of the house of lords to the correspondence of Lord George Germain and Generals Clinton and Cornwallis, and the admirals on the American station, and between these last, should not diminish the merit of this expedition

In the French translation of this correspondence, printed at Berne, in 1782, we read that the affairs of the rebels (p 52) were in such a desperate state, according to intercepted letters of their generals, that nothing but the success of some extraordinary enterprise could give vigor and activity to their cause That New York was the object of this enterprise, that the generals and the minister congratulated themselves (p 180) as if sure of repulsing it; that the Count de Grasse's orders (p. 252) were to send ten or twelve of his vessels to

November, they were asked of the governor, under an express promise to restore them to him, and they were embarked on the fleet to avoid the delays of a convoy.

It remained now to obtain cash; the merchant of the cape would give it only on two conditions: first, that some men-of-war should be detached to escort their convoy to Europe; second, that security should be given for the reimbursement. The admiral refused the first article, because, at the moment, he did not wish to enfeeble his fleet; for the second, he offered to pledge his own plantation in the island. M. de Charitte, captain of a ship-of-the-line, also offered his; they were accepted; but the money was not forthcoming and time was lost.

It was then necessary to have recourse to the same Spanish commissary (Senor de Salavedra), but he remarked that the gallions had sailed to Europe; the admiral urged him so much, that he agreed to go to

---

North America, and to furnish an escort to the merchant convoys to Europe, that the French and American army consisted of merely six thousand regular troops (p 166, 173 and 227) and the corps under M de la Fayette of 1800 mountaineers, that the militia were scarcely armed, and such as had any, badly armed, that the French could bring only slight reinforcements from the cape According to his picture, the minister, generals and admirals believed that they had nothing to fear, and the minister did not doubt (p 54) but that Admiral Rodney would reach the American coast before the Count de Grasse, and Rodney wrote (p 282) that *Admiral Hood, whom he detached there with fifteen ships, after joining Admiral Graves, would be in force sufficient to defeat the enemy and overthrow all his designs; which I have no doubt will be the case*

Havana, with his letters to the governor, and to do his best to assist the public treasury by the purses of individuals. It must be said, to the honor of the colonists, that all were eager to do so; ladies, even, offering their diamonds. Then the frigate *Concorde* was sent, on the 28th of July, to announce the coming of the fleet with reinforcements to North America.[1] To reach it, the fleet took an extraordinary route, the sense of which we afterwards saw; there was dread, doubtless, lest the frigate sent to Havana for money should be taken or not arrive soon enough; moreover, had the fleet gone by the ordinary channels, the enemy might have been informed of its course and got to the Chesapeake before it; the *Aygrette* frigate was accordingly sent to Havana. The fleet followed by the old channel, the famous dreaded channel, where no French fleet had ever passed; it set sail from the cape, August 5; on the 9th, it took coast pilots at the port of Baracoa, on the 17th, the frigate *Aygrette* rejoined it, on the 19th, the whole fleet, having passed the channel without accident, sent back the pilots; and on the 24th, being off Charleston, the cutter *la Mouche* was sent to Europe with intelligence.

The fleet had provided for the secresy of its arrival by the capture of all the enemy's corvettes and vessels it fell in with; they were, moreover, much more use-

---

[1] The letter of De Grasse to Rochambeau will be found in the Appendix S.

ful than could be imagined, in transporting the troops, after the complete destruction which Lord Cornwallis had made of the American vessels on both shores of the bay.

On the 30th of August Cape Henry was discovered N. W. ¼ W. Chesapeake Bay was reconnoitred, and the fleet anchored behind Cape Henry on the 31st. Thus, on the day named, Lord Cornwallis could no longer hope to return to New York, or derive any aid from there.

On the 1st of September, storms prevented the landing of the troops, which was to be made at Jamestown, on James river, as concerted by the admiral with the French officer (M. de Gimat) sent to Cape Henry to report the respective positions.

The English army was posted at Yorktown on York river, and thought only of fortifying itself there, unable to foresee the fate that awaited it. The Marquis de la Fayette camped at the fork of the Pamunky and Mattapony, with detachments on both sides of York river; the Pennsylvanians were on James river; the militia were assembled on the Roussock.[1] It was while this was going on that the fleet appeared at the mouth of the bay. Then General Wayne was to pass James

---

[1] Maryland, Pennsylvania, and Virginia militia were then serving, but the militia here referred to are doubtless the Virginia militia under Gov. Nelson, and the river the Rappahannock. Gov. Nelson took part in the siege and directed the gunners to fire at a prominent house which, he said, must be head quarters or something of the kind. It was his own house and still stands, bearing the marks of balls

river, and advance so as to hold the English in check, if they attempted to fall back into Carolina; but, as he had no transports to carry out this essential operation, the fleet supplied him.

On the 2d of September the weather permitted the vessels destined to carry and escort the troops to be landed (the Marquis de St. Simon, commandant,) to start from the anchorage for Jamestown; after landing the troops, they transported General Wayne and his division.[1] The *Aigrette* (M. de Traversay, captain,) returned with two prizes, a corvette of twenty-two guns, and a schooner. The *Triton* and *Vaillant* entered the river, and the *Aigrette*, the next day, took two vessels of the same kind as the previous day.

On the evening of the same day, M. du Portail,[2] a French officer, dispatched by Generals Washington and Rochambeau, announced the departure of the squadron of Count de Barras, escorting the artillery and munitions necessary for the projected siege; he was also directed to ask the assistance of the light vessels of the fleet, to enable the army, on arriving at Baltimore, to come down the Elk by water; the admiral, in the absence of his boats, ordered the ves-

---

[1] The troops landed Sept 1st, at Col. Burril's on the Isle of Wight, and St. Simon and his officers were received by Col Butler and Col. Stewart of Pennsylvania.—*Butler's Journal S.*

[2] He arrived from Newport to put himself under the orders of his junior, the Count de Grasse. No one was astonished He is of a disposition to sacrifice all considerations, at all times, to the good of the service

sels of his fleet under 64's to prepare for this service; they were ready to sail September 5th, when the enemy's fleet was signalled It had been necessary to post ships-of-the-line at the mouth of the James and York to blockade by sea Lord Cornwallis's army and all the transports attached to his army; these had to be left at their stations; thus the fleet, reduced to twenty-four vessels, had orders to form, at noon, a line in order of swiftness, the tide favoring it at that hour. This movement was executed with such precision and boldness, in spite of the absence of the best drilled part of the crew, that the enemy, doubtless taken by surprise, at once wore so as to be on the same tack as the French fleet: it had the cape E. and E. N. E.; in this position, being to leeward, it awaited the enemy's attack. The issue of the expedition, the vacancy left by the crews employed in the debarkation, the fear of getting too far from the mouths of the York and James rivers, and the fear lest the English fleet, by its known superior sailing, should succeed in getting between these mouths and the French fleet, all obliged it to keep on the defensive; the enemy held the weather-gage in excess; their balls did not come near enough to the French to receive a reply; there was no appearance that the combat would become very warm, but the winds ordered otherwise; they shifted till they came to the northeast and forced the English to attack. The two vans having come so close as to be almost within pistol shot, the fire was long well sustained, and the affair seemed about to be decisive, when Admiral Hood made a signal to the English rear division, which he commanded to bear down on the French rear. The admiral witnessed this movement with pleasure, and prepared to tack his whole fleet together, bearing N. N. W., which would inevitably have thrown the English line into confusion, but Admiral Graves anticipated him, and signalled his whole fleet to keep the wind. The heads of the two fleets gradually fell off in consequence of this new order of the English admiral, and the fire ceased at 6½, P. M.

The French fleet passed the night in the presence of the enemy in line of battle, the fires in all the vessels lighted. These signs of victory were not belied in the morning, for we perceived by the sailing of the English that they had suffered greatly; so that during the night of the 9th–10th, they had to blow up the *Terrible*, 64, themselves, and another put into the Hook in a most wretched plight.[1]

The two fleets, in sight of each other, spent the 6th of September in repairing, favored by the calm or rather by the feeble north wind that continued till 4 o'clock. The wind then came from the southwest, and the French availed themselves of it to approach the enemy. It was too late to engage again, and they lay that night as the preceding.

---

[1] Admiral Graves's letter, Sept 21 His fleet, he said, was so disabled that he could not say when he could put to sea.

On the 7th of September at day-break, the French fleet veered and tacked together to attack the head of the enemy's line; he made his van take the opposite tack; as the second English vessel wore, the French van had orders to use all efforts against the enemy; but the English fleet wore and formed in line of battle behind the last vessel. This movement withdrew the English from the French, who, to sail along the enemy's line, were unable to come up except by edging away while the English had studding sails. The variable winds and storms that sprung up in every direction, then separated the two fleets.

On the 8th of September the wind was very fresh, and the fleets kept far apart. The English held the north, and it was precisely from this direction that the French expected the squadron of M. de Barras from Newport. It was very essential to gain the weather-gage of the enemy, to prevent his revenging himself upon that squadron, composed of only seven ships of the line and one of 50; it escorted all the siege artillery, an object of vital importance. The fleet sailed northward, and at 6, P. M., the enemy lay N. N. W., and N. W. The weather-gage thus gained, the French fleet hoped to preserve it to engage in the morning; but the enemy's fleet instantly wore. At 8, P. M., it made signals, and it was thought that they wished to try and get into Chesapeake Bay before us, the more so as on the 6th two frigates detached from the English fleet had entered at full sail.

While the fleets were observing each other, the wind fell during the night, and in the morning, Sept. 9th, a squadron was discovered, though its flag could not be distinguished. The French fleet bore down on it in line of battle; but lost sight of it during the day. It was the squadron of M. de Barras, which anchored on the 10th in Chesapeake Bay. On the same day the French fleet no longer discovering anything, took its route for the same bay, where it anchored the 11th; two English frigates, the *Iris* and *Richmond*, those detached from the enemy's fleet on the 6th, were taken as they were getting out to rejoin it, by the *Aigrette* and *Diligente*, which were chasing in front of the fleet. They paid dearly for the petty advantage of cutting the buoys which the fleet had left at the anchorage, on hoisting sail Sept. 5.

All the boats and crews came on board, as soon as the return of the fleet was announced in the bay; they had remained, while waiting in James river, under the protection of the vessels anchored at its mouth. They were sent back to transport promptly the American and French army to the common rendezvous for the siege of Yorktown and Gloucester. M. de Barras, on his arrival in the bay, had detached for the same service the small craft attached to his squadron.

On the 17th Generals Washington and Rochambeau came on board the *Ville de Paris* to concert further operations.¹ As they left, they were heard expatiating on the admiral's zeal for the common cause, and his readiness in detaching a part of the marines of his vessels to augment the army of the besiegers.²

On the 20th the fleet changed its anchorage, to come nearer the army;³ it entered the bay further, more in reach of York river, and anchored in battle order reversed at its mouth, with the Horse Shoe banks in front. By this position it at once preserved to the army free communication with all the rivers flowing into the bay, and was less likely to drag the anchors or break the cables than at the other anchorage.

Although the operations of the army on land had the success which the fleet had prepared and secured them, they entered only summarily in the naval campaign; homage is due however on all occasions to the combined French and American army for the concert and harmony which reigned between two such different nations, for their ardor and noble emulation in all instances, principally during the siege of York-

---

[1] "I am happy to inform congress, that I found the French admiral disposed in the best manner to give us all the assistance in his power, and perfectly to coöperate with me in our present attempt."— *Washington to President of Congress*, 23 Sept., 1781. S

[2] These marines were really given very reluctantly on Oct. 4, when 2,000 landed on the Gloucester side.—*Sparks's Washington*, viii, 168 note, and *Butler's Journal*. S

[3] This movement was the result of a correspondence between Washington and De Grasse, which has too intimate a connection with the campaign to be omitted here. The letters will be found in the appendix. S

town;[1] a siege ever memorable for its results and for the accurate combinations, which brought together on the appointed day, a fleet coming seven hundred leagues, and a land army that had two hundred to march.

Lord Cornwallis, invested on all sides, wished in vain to try to escape from the fleet with a part of his transports, that had taken refuge under his guns. Before concluding to capitulate, he also tried to burn at their anchorage, the vessels that blockaded the mouth of the river, by sending fire-ships from Yorktown; but this had been foreseen, and the vessels gave them free passage.

The last resource having also failed, the English general asked to capitulate on the 17th of October, the same day that General Burgoyne surrendered in 1777. As soon as congress received the intelligence, its joy and its gratitude to the commanders was expressed in most authentic testimonials. The following resolutions were passed at Philadelphia, October 29th.

Resolved, That the thanks of the United States in Congress assembled, be presented to his excellency the Count de Rochambeau, for the cordiality, zeal, judgment, and fortitude, with which he seconded and advanced the progress of the allied army against the British garrison in York.

---

[1] This testimony of a naval officer is the more generous, as the army alone received favors at court; if the fleet received no mark of satisfaction, it was doubtless sufficiently rewarded by the honorable resolutions of congress

Resolved, That the thanks of the United States in Congress assembled, be presented to his excellency Count de Grasse, for his display of skill and bravery in attacking and defeating the British fleet off the Bay of Chesapeake, and for his zeal and alacrity in rendering, with the fleet under his command, the most effectual and distinguished aid and support to the allied army in Virginia

Resolved, That the United States in Congress assembled, will cause to be erected at York in Virginia, a marble column, adorned with emblems of the alliance between the United States and his most Christian Majesty; and inscribed with a succinct narrative of the surrender of Earl Cornwallis to his excellency General Washington, commander in chief of the combined forces of America and France; to his excellency the Count de Rochambeau, commanding the auxiliary troops of his most Christian Majesty in America, and his excellency the Count de Grasse, commanding in chief the naval army of France in Chesapeake.

Resolved, That two pieces of the field ordnance, taken from the British army under the capitulation of York, be presented by the commander in chief of the American army, to Count de Rochambeau; and that there be engraven thereon a short memorandum, that Congress were induced to present them from consideration of the illustrious part which he bore in effectuating the surrender.

Resolved, That the Secretary of Foreign Affairs be directed to request the Minister Plenipotentiary of his Most Christian Majesty to inform his Majesty, that it is the wish of Congress, that Count de Grasse may be permitted to accept a testimony of their approbation, similar to that to be presented to Count de Rochambeau."

    (Signed.)   Thompson."

These resolutions fully meet the charge made against the Count de Grasse, of having wished to peril the success of that expedition by a new sea fight; as this imputation rests solely on the reply of the American general to the French admiral, which has been published in Europe without adding the latter's letters, we may infer that the publication of the one without the other, and the silence of all the European gazettes as to the resolutions of congress relative to the Count de Grasse, have the same source and the same object; hence it seems just to give the motives of his letter, which we all knew.

We heard from all sides, of the speedy return of the English fleet to the Chesapeake, to engage us if the siege had not been terminated. This engagement the Count de Grasse must accept either at anchor or under sail; he explained to General Washington, that he preferred to fight under sail; laying before him his reasons drawn from scientific rules, and the position of his fleet between the mouth of a river and a bar, which would not permit him to pursue the enemy quickly enough if victorious, nor manœuvre during the engagement, if he did not first leave that anchorage; now he might well believe that the fleet would cover the siege as well, and perhaps better when under sail, than at anchor. Why then reproach him with wishing to compromise the siege? Was not the project of laying it his own? Could he wish it to fail? He had sacrificed his own glory to the good of this project on the 5th of September, when he returned to his anchorage instead of pursuing the enemy, whom he had repulsed; he sacrificed it also on this occasion, by yielding to General Washington's desire, and remaining at an anchorage where, if he did not fear being defeated, he was absolutely sure of deriving no advantage from victory.

On the 22d October the generals of the land forces came to the admiral to concert all the arrangements to be taken for the security of their conquest and the departure of the forces.

According to the report of the officers present, General Washington welcomed the Count de Grasse with cordiality and expressions attesting the decisive services which the latter had rendered his country, and the sentiments which he personally entertained for him. During the dinner given on the *Ville de Paris* to the generals and all the officers of their suite, the fleet was dressed with flags, and the health of the king, the congress, and the commanders were drunk with salvos. The American general offered one for American Independence, which, he said, was now too firm to be shaken.

The *Surveillante* set sail the 23d to carry to France the army and navy officers, chosen to bear to the king the tidings of the success of his arms. The *Andromaque* was about to hoist sail on the 28th to carry duplicates of the same dispatches; but returned into the bay, the frigates on the watch having signalled the English fleet: on the morning of the 29th thirty-one sails could be already made out off Cape Charles; by evening forty-four were signalled; the 30th they made various manœuvres, sometimes on one tack, sometimes on the other; at last at 3 they stood on the larboard tack with the wind on the quarter, and we saw no more of them.

We were at first much astonished at receiving no order to hoist sail as soon as possible, when the enemy were first signalled; but we learned that this too was in deference to the generals on land, who had expressly requested it.

The *Andromaque* sailed on the 2d of November and on the 4th, the fleet to the number of 35 ships, proceeded to double Cape Henry, and on the 5th steered for the Windward Isles. Four of these vessels under M. le Chevalier d'Albert Saint-Hippolyte, captain of a ship of the line, separated on the 9th to proceed to St. Domingo.

The remaining thirty-one anchored at Fort Royal,

Martinique, on the 26th, the day remarkable for the surprise of St. Eustatius.

The fleet needed great repairs, but did not find all that was needed at Martinique. It spent twenty days in rerigging as well as it could, and in taking in provisions: by the help of neutral vessels, it set sail December 17, badly enough prepared; since its departure from Brest, Europe having furnished it neither masts, extras of any kind nor sailors; sickness, engagements and desertion had diminished the crews more than five thousand men.

The fleet had orders to get to windward of Martinique, by plying to windward in the channel of St. Lucia. to reach it more easily, every vessel was at liberty to manœuvre independently. Although the wind was always contrary and in squalls, several vessels got to windward; but the force of the currents augmented by that of the squalls, drove them back into the channel and prevented the others from getting to windward Accidents multiplied and the fleet per force put back to Martinique and anchored in the roadstead of Fort Royal, December 24th. The crews were exhausted with the forced labor of this fruitless cruise. The fleet set sail again the 28th, met the same difficulty and returned to the same roadstead the appointed rallying place. The event which brought it back had been foreseen, but it wished to hasten to profit by its superiority which it was not much longer to enjoy. Moreover it could get on the

17th December provisions for only forty-seven days; it feared that the convoys, impatiently expected, would not arrive in that time: hence an attack must be made on some hostile island, if only to procure subsistence a little longer.

In consequence, the weather continuing unfavorable to reach Barbadoes, we started January 5th, for St. Christopher's with 26 ships of the line (the others were refitting) and 6,000 land troops divided among the ships and transports. We hoped to find subsistence in that island, draw the enemy to leeward to defend it, and thus divert them from attacking the convoys from France, which had been too long expected not to arrive soon.

The fleet hove to off St. Christopher's on the 11th, and the next day anchored at the Basse Terre of that island. scarcely had it cast anchor when the whole island submitted; the inhabitants deputed their chief men and capitulated for the whole island, except the high, precipitous, and well fortified rock called Brimstone Hill, situated on the southwest of the island, to which the garrison retired quite precipitately.

On the same day, the 12th, all the troops were landed, and by night Brimstone Hill was invested. The artillery was landed next day; and mortar batteries soon established; but when a breach was to be made the first battery of 24 of the *Caton* was taken for the service.

During the siege, the most difficult in America,

from the position and nature of this rock, Admiral Hood came to the relief of the island with twenty-two vessels and a body of land troops; he was signalled the 24th, and the French fleet at once set sail to meet him. Had we remained at anchor, the army on land would have lost all communication with the neighboring islands, a necessary communication for its subsistence rendered precarious by the delay of the convoys from Europe; moreover it could not have rallied the vessels that were to join it, after repairing at Martinique. In fact the *Hector* came in the same day.

The French fleet formed in line of battle in the natural order: it came in sight of the enemy only the next day at day break under the isle of Monserrat, which had not yet capitulated. The English tacked to approach St. Christopher's and endeavored to avoid an action as much as the French endeavored to come up with them; but the English had the weather-gage, and could not but have it, the attacked island being to leeward; it varied in the direction of E. S. E., which facilitated their standing with a free wind towards St. Christopher's, while it obliged the French to hug the wind so as to press the enemy on Isle Nevis. The French light squadron and van had orders to bear down on the enemy's, which had gone in a line with that island; the rest of the French fleet kept the wind, and, in consequence of its direction, was in a bow and quarter line; at this moment the French light squadron instead of continuing to bear down on the enemy, bore away. The admiral, surprised at this manœuvre, thought that Nevis intercepted their wind; to assure himself of it, he signalled him to lie to, which the squadron did; assured by this that it was by no fault of wind that they bore away, the admiral repeated his first signal to the squadron and the van; but it was too late, the English fleet, favored by the wind, superior in sailing qualities, being all copper fastened, took the resolution of hurrying towards St. Christopher's; and although the French fleet made every effort to overtake his rear, which it even handled roughly, it could not prevent the enemy anchoring near the spot from which it had sailed. Then it took the larboard tack to stand out to sea, and prepared to attack the English the next day at this anchorage.

The English admiralty has published an extract of a letter of Admiral Hood's, giving an account of this affair; it contains a boast good enough for the London mob, but which can not come from an officer so distinguished for his talents; he seems to attach a sort of triumph to occupying the same anchorage that the French had before the engagement. This is an illusion easily destroyed; this anchorage could not be the same, although on the same shore, because the English fleet would there have been exposed to the fire of the land batteries. The most important anchorage for the English admiral, the only one decisive for raising the siege of Brimstone Hill, could he have taken it and held his ground there, was that of Sandy

Point: there, even under sail, he could have communicated directly with the fortress, he could have landed his troops under his guns, and been protected by them in case of attack; the place would never have been totally invested; for the English troops landed by Admiral Hood from his anchorage, and whom he was forced to reëmbark, might have occupied the post which the cannon of Brimstone Hill obliged Mr. Duchilleau to abandon: hence at Sandy Point they might have communicated with the besieged place, and with their squadron, and the position of the besiegers would have become very critical, on the other hand the vaunted anchorage, if it favored the landing of the English troops, could not have been more useful to their project than it was, because it was too far from the besieged place, and the English corps was too weak to cut its way through to it. Thus the French fleet being under sail to windward of the English, the latter had simply taken the most hazardous position, from which a circumstance beyond its knowledge, alone, as we shall see, delivered it.

On the 26th at 7, A. M., the fleet rallied in the natural order of battle, on the starboard tack; at 7½ it had orders to clear for action: the French van attacked the enemy's rear, several vessels of which lay far from each other and from the rest of their fleet; the fire of the French obliged them to hoist sail precipitately to gain a higher roadstead: the French vessels at the head having veered in succession, the line was in natural, order on the larboard tack. The winds being from E. to E. S. E., another tack enabled the French to attack the English rear a second time; but only the head of the French line could come into action, and the wind prevented the action from becoming general.

We should have attacked again on the 27th, if the English squadron had not appeared out of reach of insult; the vessels cut up the day before were removed and eight or nine of the largest had taken their places. They were anchored, the bowsprit of one over the stern of the other; thus unattackable, the fleet contented itself with keeping them there.

On the 28th the frigates informed the admiral that the enemy's position, as they lay at anchor with springs on the cables, was a perfect chain formed by their twenty-two men of war, the first of which was so anchored that no one could pass ahead of it; the rear forming the angle of the line enclosed their frigates and other small craft; in consequence we contented ourselves with so completely intercepting all communication from the seaward that Admiral Hood was forced to send and ask a passport of the French admiral to dispatch his wounded to Antigua.

On the 29th the English land forces disembarked; and having been repulsed with great loss, reembarked. The *Triomphant*, Marquis de Vaudreuil, and *Brave*, Count d'Ambliment, arrived from Brest on the 4th of February. By them we learnt the mischance that befel the convoy of which they formed part, and we inferred that Admiral Hood knew it before he came to endeavor to relieve St. Christopher's, as he had not preferred to go and await the convoy at the landing places.

On the 12th Brimstone Hill proposed to capitulate, and the 13th the French garrison took possession.

The forces had taken on the 17th of December, provisions for only forty-seven days, being all that could be supplied. For the last ten days they were maintained only by the prizes taken at St. Christopher's, or from the neutral vessels which it had been forced to stop; the munitions of war were not more plentiful, several vessels had not enough to live on for thirty-six hours or fight with for two; fortunately provisions from the Mediterranean had reached Martinique; and it was announced to the fleet to its great satisfaction, that it should receive them at Nevis on the 14th. To render the delivery more prompt and convenient, it proceeded to anchor off the town of that name, a league or a league and a half from the head of the English fleet; the latter might have been deceived by the number of small vessels, and taken them for fire ships intended for it, so that while the French fleet was providing for its urgent necessities, necessities more imperious than the duty of fighting, the English squadron cut their cables during the night; and the better to conceal their course made no signals; and falling to leeward ran under St. Eustatius to retire with all haste.

The French fleet asked nothing better than to engage the English, when it left the conquered island; but it was out of provisions and the admiral could not prevent the English executing their manœuvre; this manœuvre necessarily led the two armies under the wind, drew the French off from their provisions, and its necessity was so great that it could not defer even for twenty-four hours taking in supplies. Now the first care of a commander is to provision his army; and the best he could do was to provision it in the surest, promptest manner, to the windward of the enemy; he did so: if the English, favored by the night, without signals, leaving his anchors, steering to leeward, putting boats at their anchorage with the same lights they were in the habit of showing, leaving their sick on their hospital ships, were fortunate enough to escape him, they owed it only to the absolute and urgent necessity of the French fleet, and not to the fault of the admiral who drew off from before the enemy only to obtain provisions, never was more than a league and a half off, kept always to windward and never out of sight of their fires, this was surely all that he could or should have done under the circumstances.

On the 16th the fleet anchored at the Basse Terre of the conquered island, and began to reembark the troops and artillery. It hoisted sail on the 22d for

Martinique, steering to leeward so as to take possession of the island of Monserrat on the way. A detachment of vessels under M. de Barras, received its capitulation on the same terms as St. Christopher's. On the night of the 26th the whole French fleet was back at the roadstead of Fort Royal.

The repairs of the vessels were constantly more numerous, difficult and long; neither means nor crews had been increased: the convoy from Europe was still expected, and a very considerable supply of masts, sails, rigging and extras of all kinds, as well as munitions and supplies were required. There was almost a new equipment to make, crews to be augmented a third, ships to careen, &c., &c. Yet the convoy escorted by the *Couronne*, brought only three ships of the line, two hundred and fifty sailors, and some transports, the *Triomphant* had brought the account of the munitions sent at its departure on each vessel, and it was easy to distinguish what was intended for the fleet from what was intended for the colony. According to the project made, the former should have followed the fleet loaded; the others should have been discharged at leisure without retarding the departure of the fleet: on the contrary the cargo of the ships escorted by the *Couronne*, had been made precipitately without a distinct detailed account: all was heaped in pell mell; all the ships had to be unloaded to ascertain which belonged to each. Had there been order, the fleet would have sailed sooner and the enemy would have been so unprepared to follow, that they would have learned its departure and the arrival of the convoy at the same time.

After the revictualling and refitting had been accelerated as much as circumstances would permit, the fleet set sail on the 8th of April.

On the 9th the English fleet approached the French, which was to windward, covering the route of its convoy towards Guadaloupe, and, the rallying of two of his vessels[1] retained by a calm near Dominica; the English van profited by the first gusts to form in line, while the rest of his fleet was still becalmed under Dominica. In this hampered position the French commander saw a chance to act on the English van; he did so successfully: their van retired before his which handled it roughly. He would probably have pursued it, had he not feared for his two vessels; he was sure of rallying them by going to meet them, and he was not sure of taking the vessels of the English van, which had been crippled: after three hours fighting the admiral took the surest course and rallied his vessels. He immediately sent orders to the convoy to continue its route towards St Domingo, which it did, setting sail again at 11, P. M.

This convoy was very embarrassing before a superior hostile fleet, all sheathed with copper, of more even and quicker sailing. It could not yet have made

---

[1] The *Chevalier de Goussencourt* says the *Auguste* and *Zélé*.

distance enough by 10, A. M.; the French fleet would have soon rejoined it and the English been better enabled to route it: thus the French continued to ply to windward in the channel of Dominica, keeping the weather-gage of the English.

On the 11th the French had almost doubled Saintes, when well founded fears arose as to two of their vessels which had sailed so that they could be intercepted by a number of the enemy's vessels, whose best sailors were giving them a lively chase; the whole French fleet had to be rallied to their relief; it thus lost most of what headway it had gained over the enemy: but it rallied the vessels, and saw those in chase fall off as quickly as possible.

Then constant to his project the French fleet resumed the weather-gage and would have soon been as far ahead of the enemy as before, had not the flag ship been run into by the *Zélé*, by a violation of the order of sailing expressly prescribed.[1] These two vessels were obliged to lay to to leeward during the whole time it took them to get loose, and the vessel which had run foul, more injured than the other, asked to be taken in tow, which was done, but, having fallen still more to leeward, made signal at daybreak that the enemy's fleet was approaching. Then the admiral, who was plying to windward to rejoin the fleet, ordered it to rally and to form in line

---

[1] This order was that "Tout batiment ayant les armures à bas bord devoit arriver, sans avoir égard à l'ancienneté."

in his wake to cover the *Zélé* in its retreat to Guadaloupe.

Those who always judge by the result, have not failed to say that the admiral should have abandoned the *Zélé* and continued his course without engaging. Had he so determined the day before and the two preceding days, he would have had three or four vessels less, at least on the 12th, and would have been justly reproached for losing ships without an engagement. There was still eight to ten days' sail; some vessels would have sailed worse than the rest or met some accident; thus without striking a blow, he would have diminished his fleet before reaching St. Domingo, more than it would be by the most disastrous battle; then all the blame would have fallen justly on the admiral, and on his bravery and not on his inferiority.

The French fleet in battle order was joined at 8, A. M., by the enemy in an order which exposed their van to be crushed by the whole French fleet, without giving time for the rest of the English fleet to prevent it. The admiral, to profit by this unwise disposition, wished his whole fleet to veer at once to bring it on the same tack as the enemy; but this movement was not executed, although it was repeated exactly and known through the whole line. It has been pretended that they were too near the enemy to wear; as though one could be too near an enemy when you wish to engage him sharply; and as though the commander's glance did not show him that what was possible for his vessel was so for the others. The order to veer in succession was no better executed, though it would have supplied the failure of the other. The admiral's rigging was totally cut up by one of the seconds of the English flag ship, another French vessel lost all her masts, the winds changed in favor of the English, the French line was cut in two places and a calm came on. As soon as the winds sprang up, they might have reformed in line and done it so as to render the English van useless in the engagement, for it was to leeward. The admiral gave the order, but in spite of all his signals a part of his fleet preferred to run before the wind and keep on obstinately, even with studding sails.

To render the history of this day clearer, requires the signals and plans before the eye: but from what has been summarily said, there is no officer in the fleet, the least competent to judge, who will not see that the first order placed us most advantageously, and that after the calm the combat might have been very honorably renewed.

At last at night, after having been constantly sustained by seven or eight vessels, the *Ville de Paris*, long since abandoned by its two seconds, without ammunition, her rigging all cut away, surrounded and cannonaded by ten English vessels, surrendered after twelve hours fight, in such a state that she had to be towed to Jamaica.

We have been told that not to be lost in Parisian circles, it would have been more becoming to blow up the flagship; one must then be more ferocious on sea than land, and in France more than in other nations. Neither law nor honor gives a captain such a right over his crew, he has only himself to kill. Fools and cowards need this means of escaping shame; but misfortune does not humiliate the brave. If the Count de Grasse escaped over three hundred cannon that swept his deck, it is clear that his destiny preserved his life only for his reputation sake; for the dead would all be wrong and the acts of the living be whitened at their expense; this was well observed at St. Domingo, where he was supposed to be certainly killed. As soon as the contrary was known, language and letters changed.

The Count de Grasse arrived at Jamaica April 29th; he was transferred on the 2d of May to Spanish town, and the 19th of the same month to the *Sandwich*, commanded by Admiral Parker, who was to escort a fleet of merchantmen to Europe. He sailed May 25th and reached Portsmouth on the 31st of July, arriving in London on the 3d of August by his Britannic majesty's orders. He had scarcely entered the lodgings prepared for him and the French officers when General Conway, by the king's orders, wished to give him a guard of honor, which he refused. Soon after high officers of the court came from his majesty to invite him to the palace of St James, to occupy the apartments prepared for him. Sensible as the Count de Grasse was to this honor, he begged his majesty to excuse his not accepting it, and leaving his comrades. An hour after the king sent to hire for him the whole house where he lodged, ordered his expenses and those of all the French officers to be defrayed during their stay in his kingdom, and at the same time announced that he expected to see him the following Friday.

On the 9th of August, he with the French officers had the honor of being presented to their Britannic majesties and the royal family, who lavished on him the most flattering marks.[1]

The visits, invitations from the ministry, the eagerness of many leading men, the crowd at his door, and wherever he passed, repeating their expressions of consideration, are no unequivocal sign in a country where actors of every order and quality are hissed and where the ignorant and the cowardly can never hope to draw the crowd

The king of England had himself given orders to Admiral Keppel to convey the Count de Grasse and the French officers to France on vessels chartered at the expense of the admiralty, as soon as they were ready He left London on the 12th, reached Calais on the 13th, and Paris on the morning of the 16th.

---

[1] The king speaking of the components of the French navy, wittily termed the intruded captains and admirals as *inspired officers*, probably with the same views on this matter as the famous Admiral De Ruyter — *Vie de Ruyter, Amsterdam,* 1698 *fol,* p 698

On the 18th the Count de Grasse presented himself before the king and obtained all that he could desire; a severe examination of his conduct and a council of war. This favor would have been complete, had the result been more prompt; many think it might have been, if, as is said, the Count de Grasse simply presents himself as captain of his vessel and admiral of the fleet without charges against any one. Lock's book and the plans of the battles are the only documents of the trial. The courage of the captain, the intelligence of the commander, are the only questions. The commanders of the fleet have then only to produce the logs and plans; as to the execution of the signals, the commander is not responsible, and this may be ample matter for another court martial.

All can feel how painful it is to languish under the public censure, for the public asks success. It must even be avowed that fortune most surely indicates the hero to the crowd, with them the fortunate are always skillful and prudent Repeated campaigns, combats, decisive success, are lost in a single day, especially if, beside the disfavor of a last misfortune, one has undergone, during the whole course of his command, a concerted system of calumny, which spared neither forged anecdotes nor false reports, nor odious suppressions nor mercenary pens to accredit them as occasion required.

Although time dispels illusions, it is no less afflicting not to enjoy one's reputation till after death, especially after having always lived more on consideration than reward; if one commits no other crime against his country than the unskillfulness or the want of discipline of his subordinates, and none against some enemies, but the honor of despising them, and the frankness of saying so.

When command has been reached only by campaigns and combats, an old sailor has often more the talent and even the roughness of the trade than the turn and grace of society; if his innocence supposes too many guilty, it thereby augments the number of those interested in his fall. Too isolated, too awkward moreover to make a party, he can have only a few gratuitous benevolent partisans.

When we reflect on destiny, the Count de Grasse might have had a more useful one. Had he been dishonored from youth, driven from his native land by public contempt, he would have gone pirating on distant shores, and then escaped only by a royal hand from the just reward with which the English repay a breach of parol, this debut might yet have closed by honors and reputation.[1]

Had he constantly had fits of baseness and hauteur, timidity and rodomontade, familiarity and indiscretion with his subalterns, dissimulation and childish jealousy with the superiors, lucid moments of counsel and reason with the rarest incoherences, some ideas

---

[1] All this alludes to d'Estaing.

at first sight, bold and luminous, always incomplete or abortive on the whole or in execution; if the project agreed on the evening had been sacrificed to the dreams of the night, it is clear that the wise and especially medical men would have sought in the animal economy the solution of all these contradictions; especially if they were told of an old disposition from birth to suppose fabulous adventures, imaginary combats, visions by night and broad day, &c. Yet some people would have taken these freaks for ideas and this folly for genius.

Then the Count de Grasse become a great man, might have left port without even looking at his masts. He might have exposed himself to perish in a neighboring gulf, lose precious time in passing the straits to range obstinately the opposite coast,[1] then throw himself into a calm so as not to follow one of the two common routes, and show on all occasions the most settled love for this bizarre and dangerous tactics against winds and coasts, that fortune would sometimes seem to have been exhausted not in giving him success, but in getting him out of scrapes.

He would always have advanced or fallen back at the wrong time, had 800 men killed in an impossible

---

[1] The Count d'Estaing sailed from Toulon, April 13, 1778, and by not putting in at Hieres was drawn into the gulf of Genoa; the squadron, poorly fitted, lost her masts, and he by the delay lost the opportunity of surprising the English in the Delaware

attack, instead of easily destroying a fleet at anchor.[1] He might indeed have taken an ill defended island and bruit about this victory which in the eyes of sensible people deserved punishment, if only for the fine occasion lost of seizing several ships of the line and a whole convoy.[2]

At last, for his final adieu, he might have gone and gratuitously sacrificed 1,500 men[3] and then deserted his fleet that in vain awaited him for several days. He would have been received none the less as a hero on his arrival, and in his happy hand all would have become victories and laurels. Be not surprised, the road to reach glory surely, is a simple one.

1st. If the Count de Grasse had entered the navy as a general, he would infallibly have decried his service to render it suspected and exceptionable The sensible people who compose it, would have cried very uselessly, that it never was a crime for a general not to have been born a soldier, nor for an admiral not to have been a sailor or midshipman. That they know wondrous well that superior people fly where others only crawl, that they have on the contrary been enraptured to see a man announced as enterprising arrive, in the hope that he might emancipate the generals from the tutelage of bureaus and cabinets,

---

[1] His action with Barrington and repulse at St Lucia

[2] St Vincent

[3] The attack on Savannah

but that it must however be avowed, that although Lucullus left Rome a great captain, we must not conclude that all the admirals who start from Paris have the same privilege.

2d. To give one's name to some fashions, figure as a sd. design, subsidize gazetteers and journalists, buy up hawkers of songs and verses, write to merchants that the art of convoying is at last discovered, that you are the only man of precaution for their interests; ask their advice and orders, and call yourself *with the most profound esteem and respect, their very humble, &c.* Then you get proclaimed in the squares of commerce, in the public papers, applauded at the opera and played on the boulevards.

But enough on the plan of fortune that his friends might have desired for the Count de Grasse; this is only a slight interest when we consider the general cause; for the navy and the whole nation is to be thought of. If all this becomes a war of pen and intrigue; if by embarrassment, management, or a false and cruel sensibility, it is sought to draw the curtain over the past, the present and the future are lost, and the 12th of April, 1782 on the first occasion will perhaps decide a battle.

If it is feared that all was not prejudged and settled, and that there were no judges, we might seek them in a rival nation, enlightened and equitable however: the peace offers a fine occasion of sending all the proceedings of the examination there, and the Hoods,

Howes, Parkers, Barringtons, Digbys, Graves, &c., will judge the cause.

Awaiting the result of an affair on which all the navies of the world keep an attentive eye, this is the testimony of a witness who has not lost sight of the flag since 1781. His grade gives no great weight to his suffrage; but as he speaks only of what he has seen, he believes he owes the testimony to his country and to truth, and he would not fear to give it or his name before the crowd of milliners, painters of tavern signs, cutlers, song hawkers, gazetteers, plagiarists, pit yellers, maids and valets of the wardrobe, courtiers of intrigue and calumny, and above all before the director and hero of the troupe.

APPENDIX.

SIEGE OF YORKTOWN, ETC.

Letter from Count de Grasse to General Washington, concerning Operations in the Chesapeake.

CAPE HENRY, 23 September, 1781

Sir,

The intelligence, which your Excellency has sent to me by the aid-de-camp of Count de Rochambeau, is most distressing. I know but little of the evil and the progress, which this operation may effect, but I perceive that our position is changed by the arrival of Admiral Digby.

The enemy is now nearly equal to us in strength, and it would be imprudent in me to place myself in a situation that would prevent my attacking them, should they attempt to afford succour. I have the honor therefore to propose to your Excellency that I should leave two vessels at the mouth of York River, and draw around me all the rest, excepting the corvettes and frigates, which have been blockading James River since my arrival, and which are the *Charlotte* the *Cormorant*, the *Sandwich* and one other frigate. The rest I shall bring together, in order to sail and keep the sea, that in case the enemy attempt to force the passage, I may attack them in a less disadvantageous position. But it is possible, that the issue of the combat may force us to leeward, and deprive us of the power of returning. Under these circumstances, what could you do, what would be your resources? I can not sacrifice the army under my command, and my present position is neither favorable for attacking, nor secure in case of a gale.

The anchorage at York, on which we were agreed, does not appear more suitable, considering the maritime forces of the enemy; because it would place me in a very unfavorable position, and would have no effect in preventing the reinforcement from entering. I see no resource but the offing, and possibly that may not leave me free to return within the Capes. I shall wait impatiently for your answer, and that of M de Rochambeau, to whom this letter is addressed in common with you. I beg you to communicate it to him, and to send your advice and opinions on the subject

If my troops, or those of M de St. Simon, remain with you, the two vessels and the corvettes at James River will be sufficient for you I will sail with my forces towards New York, and I may possibly do more for the common cause than by remaining here an idle spectator. If the enemy do not come out, it is evidently because they dare not. We shall then consider what course to take. In the meantime you will push Cornwallis vigorously, and we will act in concert, each on his own side I have the honor to be, with respectful consideration, &c.

COUNT DE GRASSE.

Letter of Gen. Washington to Count de Grasse.

WILLIAMSBURGH, 22 September, 1781.

Sir,

The enclosed letter for your Excellency, and the copies of others to Count de Rochambeau and myself, have this moment come to my hands. I deem the intelligence they contain of so much importance, that I have thought it proper to transmit them immediately to you by the Baron Closen, one of the aids-de-camp to Count de Rochambeau.[1] I am, dear Sir, &c

———o———

This letter, sustained by the explanations and arguments of the Marquis de Lafayette, produced a change in the schemes of Count de Grasse; and he agreed to remain within the Capes, and blockade the bay during the siege. He laid the matter before a council of war. "The result has been" said he in his reply, "that the plan I had suggested was the most brilliant and glorious, but it would not fulfil the views we had proposed. It is consequently decided, that a large part of the fleet shall anchor in York River, that four or five vessels shall be stationed so as to pass up and down in James River, and that you shall aid us with the means to erect a battery on Point Comfort, where we can place cannon and mortars. We shall immediately proceed to execute this arrangement, and I hasten to give you notice, that we may act in concert for the advancement of our operations."

———o———

Account of de Grasse's Conquest of Tobago, from the Gazette de France, Aug. 10, 1781.

The king's fleet, commanded by the Count de Grasse, had gained Martinico the 28th of April. In the afternoon they descried the enemy's fleet. At 8 in the evening the admiral learned that Fort Royal was blocked up by seventeen English ships and five frigates or other light vessels. The next morning at break of day, the fleet steered for Fort Royal with its convoy, and at half past eleven the two fleets were within cannon shot. The engagement began, and the Count de Grasse gave orders for the convoy to put into Fort Royal, whilst the two fleets

---

[1] The intelligence contained in the letters was, that Admiral Digby had just arrived at New York with a reinforcement of six ships of the line.

were engaged. From the beginning of the action the enemy crowded sail; the French pursued them thirty leagues to the westward of St. Lucia; and having no hopes of coming up with them, returned to Martinico, where the fleet anchored the 6th of May

The Sieur Fournier de Bellevue, lieutenant, died of the wound he received in the engagement. The Sieur de Perigny of the marine guard had an arm shot off

As soon as the Count de Grasse was joined by the Marquis de Bouillé, Governor General of Martinico, they concerted together an expedition against the island of Tobago; but in order to conceal that operation, and take off the enemy's attention, it was agreed to make a false attack, with 1,500 men on St. Lucia.

In consequence of this project the Marquis de Bouillé set out the 8th of May, with the troops for the false attack, and the squadron sailed the 9th with a reinforcement of troops; those destined to attack the island of Tobago under the command of the Sieur de Blanchelande, went off at the same time under the protection of the ships *le Pluton* and *la Serapis*, commanded by Count d'Albert de Rions On the 10th at midnight, the troops were landed under the fire of the batteries of Gros Islet of St. Lucia, the enemy's cannon did no damage nor occasioned any loss. At 2 o'clock the troops were on land, and the boats under sail; the fleet to the windward of St Lucia covered the expedition The guard was surprised, the sentinel killed, and an officer and 94 soldiers taken, who occupied the town of Gros Islet.

The Marquis de Bouillé, informed of the position of the enemy, who had fallen back to their posts, and being well informed that the Morne Fortuné could not be taken, because the island had received a reinforcement of 600 men two days before, made his troops reëmbark the 12th in the night, to the number of 1,500 men, leaving only 2 behind, who had strayed in the island; and bringing away with him 120 prisoners, a great number of muskets, clothing, &c.

The fleet cruised till the 15th, to windward of St. Lucia; it then returned to Fort Royal; the Marquis de Bouillé embarked on board of it with 8,000 men; the 25th it put to sea, and the 30th, in the morning, was in sight of the island of Tobago

They discovered some enemy's ships to windward, it was a division of six ships, with as many transports, that were going to the relief of that island; that division was chased by our fleet, but could come up with only one vessel on the lookout, which was taken.

The Sieur de Blanchelande had happily effected his debarkation the 24th, under cover of the ships, the *Pluto* and the *Experiment*, which had driven the enemy from the battery, he had taken the town of Scarborough, and a little fort that protected it; but the English had entrenched themselves on a very high mountain, with cannon, provisions and 800 men

The 31st, the Marquis du Chilleau landed with the battalion of Viennoit, at Man of War bay, to windward of the island; the Marquis de Bouillé disembarked with the battalion of Dillon and 300 grenadiers and chasseurs of the regiments of Armagnac and Auxerrois, in Courland bay; the Count de Dillon, the Count de Damoy, and the Marquis de Livarot, landed with the rest of the troops

The Marquis de Bouillé having marched to Scarborough, found there the troops commanded by the Sieur de Blanchelande, in sight of the enemy, who had intrenched themselves on the Morne Fortuné to the number of 3 or 400 troops, and 4 or 500 militia, a number of negro chasseurs, seven pieces of cannon, and two obitzers. It was decided to attack that post with 2,000 men, who were assembled in a moment under the command of the Marquis de Bouillé

The Morne Concorde was abandoned in the night. the enemy being informed of the arrival of the French troops, were in full march, after having spiked up their guns; the van of our troops pursued them, and all the rest soon followed, the Viscount de Dames had orders to take post on the Morne Concorde

The enemy was pursued a whole day, the heat was excessive,

the roads bad, and strewed with English soldiers dead or dying of fatigue: the French troops could no longer stand it, and there remained only about 150 chasseurs of Walsh and Royal Comtois in the van guard, when they came up with the English troops who had halted in a defile.

Major Ferguson, commandant general of the island, then capitulated; and on the 2d of June, the governor and the garrison laid down their arms and their standards.

The garrison consisted of about 400 men of the 86th regiment and of the artillery, 300 of which were embarked on board of the French ships; between 4 and 500 Scotchmen composed the militia, which was very fine and equal to regular troops.

We have not yet an exact account of the stores taken; it is estimated that there must be 50 pieces of large cannon, seven field pieces and two brass obitzers

---

Journal of the Operations of the Fleet under Count de Grasse, abridged from the Gazette de France of the 20th of November.

[Almon's Remembrancer, XIII, 46]

Comte de Grasse after a very short passage from Brest, arrived the 29th of April, off Martinico, whence he drove off 18 English ships of the line, which had blockaded that place for the space of 50 days As they had the advantage both of wind and swiftness, the comte was obliged to drop the chase, and enter Fort Royal. A feint attack was made upon St Lucia, when the real intention was to take Tobago, which colony was reduced, in the very sight even of Rodney himself, who, with 22 ships against 24, was pleased to stand an unconcerned spectator, keeping an awful distance, and constantly refusing coming to action, which the French offered him with a good grace The 5th of August, the fleet weighed anchor from St

Domingo, and on the 30th arrived in the Bay of Chesapeak. The dispatches of Generals Washington and Rochambeau, received by Comte de Grasse, informed him of the situation of their army, and the success which the British arms had obtained in Virginia and Maryland. The frigate *Concorde*, by which the intelligence had been conveyed, was sent back to acquaint the above generals that the French fleet was arrived off Cape Henry. Here the comte took up 3,300 men, under the command of Marquis St Simon, and distributed them on board the 28 ships of war which composed his fleet. Comte Barras, informed of the disposition, and thinking that his union with the Comte de Grasse would be of the greatest service, cheerfully renounced the superior command which he had in the northern parts, and sailed for the Chesapeake. The *Glorieux*, the *Aigrette*, and the *Diligente*, sailed before the fleet and took the advice boat *Loyalist*. The *Glorieux* dropped anchor at the mouth of the river York and next day being reinforced by the *Vaillant* and the *Triton*, the river James was also shut up, and every means taken to prevent the retreat of Lord Cornwallis to Carolina. Marquis Saint Simon, with his 3,300 men, arrived at the head of the river James, on the 2d of September the Marquis de La Fayette on the 3d, with a body of troops under his command, and on the 4th they proceeded to Williamsburgh five leagues from York. The fleet moored at Lynn Haven, was waiting for intelligence concerning the march of General Washington; as also the return of their boats and sloops, when on the 5th the enemy's fleet was descried bearing down to the Chesapeake with crowded sails. Comte de Grasse instantly dispatched orders to recall the rowing boats, which were taking in water, and directed the fleet to be in readiness for weighing, which was effected by noon, when they formed themselves in a line.

Notwithstanding the absence of 1,800 men and 90 officers employed in landing the troops, in less than three quarters of an hour, the whole line was formed in the following order *Pluto, Bourgogne, Marseillois, Diadême, Refléchi, Auguste,*

Saint Esprit, Caton, Cæsar, Destin, Ville de Paris, Victoire, Sceptre, Northumberland, Palmier, Solitaire, Citoyen, Scipion, Magnanime, Hercule, Languedoc, Zélé, Hector, and *Souverain* The enemy had kept the wind, forming themselves in a line upon the starboard tack. At 2 o'clock they tacked altogether on the same tack with us, without being, nevertheless, drawn out in parallel line; the rear of Admiral Graves being infinitely to the windward of his van, the headmost ships of the French fleet were by the current, too far to windward, to keep in a regular line. At 4 o'clock the action began at the van commanded by Sieur de Bougainville, with a very brisk fire, and successively all the ships of the main body came in for their share. At 5, the wind having continued in its variation, the French van still remained too far to windward: that of Admiral Graves was very ill treated, and this officer improved the advantage of the wind, to keep at a distance, and avoid being attacked by the French rear The setting of the sun terminated this combat

The 7th, at noon, the wind shifted favorably for the French fleet. Comte de Grasse drew near to the enemy, and manœuvred during the evening, in order to keep the wind in the night The 8th at the dawn, Admiral Graves improved a favorable gale, in an endeavor to gain the wind of the French In the evening of the 9th, Comte de Grasse, by a skillful manœuvre had the great advantage of being able to crowd more sail, his ships having suffered much less than those of the English squadron; but in the night the enemy disappeared. Comte de Grasse seeing the difficulty there was of forcing Admiral Graves to an action, and fearing, lest by means of some favorable wind, the enemy would get before him to the Chesapeake, returned thither to continue his operations. The 11th, the two frigates *Richmond* and *Iris*, which sailed the evening before from the bay, where they had been to cut off the buoys of the fleet of the Comte de Grasse, fell into his hands.

The French fleet, in the affair of the 5th, consisted of 24 ships of war and two frigates. Admiral Graves, reinforced by

Hood, had 20 sail of the line, two of them three deckers, and nine frigates and advice boats; according to their own account, five of their principal ships were considerably damaged, and especially the *Terrible*, of 74 guns, the sixth ship of the line, which they set on fire on the 9th at night; as it was impossible to keep her above water. The 15 ships first above mentioned, in the French line were all that were engaged, and opposed to the same number of the enemy's ships; five of the English rear having refused to come within reach. The French fleet on this occasion lost Capt. Boades of the *Réfléchi;* Lieut. Dufe d'Orvault major of the blue squadron; Rhaal, a Swede and midshipman on board the *Caton;* de la Villeon, auxiliary officer on board the *Diademe*, 180 wounded; in all killed and wounded, 200.

Meanwhile the combined armies of America and France had reached the mouth of Elk river, the van guard under the command of Comte de Custine, who had embarked on board country vessels arrived at Williamsburgh the 19th, the rest of the army, commanded by Baron de Viomesnil having marched as far as Baltimore, took shipping there, on board frigates and transports sent by Comte de Grasse. On the 24th they all met at Williamsburgh, there Generals Washington and Rochambeau had arrived on the 13th by land, having only two aids de camp in their train. On the 18th the generals went on board the *Ville de Paris*, in order to consult with Comte de Grasse on the best methods to be pursued. The French admiral left Lynn Haven, where the ships could not be safe, and went to that which is above Milbank ground and Horseshoe, where they dropped anchor in a line in order to prevent Admiral Graves, now reinforced by the arrival of Admiral Digby, from giving any assistance to Lord Cornwallis. Three ships were also appointed to shut up the entrance of James river. On the 31st 800 men from the marines were sent as a reinforcement to the Sieur de Choisy, who then blockaded Gloucester, with the Duke of Lauzun's legion and 2,000 Americans. Yorktown was invested on the 29th and the trench on the 7th of October, P M. On the 17th Lord Cornwallis desired a suspension of hostilities for 24 hours (General Burgoyne had signed four years ago on the same day, the convention of Saratoga). Two hours were granted him, and then he made overtures for capitulation. A whole day was taken up in debating about the articles, which at length were concluded and signed the 19th.

In the posts of York and Gloucester were found 6,000 regulars, English and Hessians; 11 pair of colors; 1,500 seamen; 106 guns of different bores, 75 of which were brass ordnance; 8 mortars; about 40 ships, 1 of them of 50 guns, which was burnt; besides 20 sail of transports which were sunk, and amongst them the frigate *Guadeloupe*.

Actions of April 9th and 12th.

The author of the *Voyage d'un Suisse dans différentes colonies d'Amerique pendant la derniere guerre*, Neuchatel, 1785, who was present at De Grasse's defeat, thus describes it:

"Admiral Rodney every day sends out some frigates, which come to the entrance of the harbor to observe us.

M. de Grasse's fleet takes incessantly all the troops here except 2,000 men who remain to defend the island And I who have obtained permission to embark on board a man of war, may hope that in such good company nothing will retard my arrival in St. Domingo

On the 7th of April, I repair to my new post, where all to my eyes seems beautiful.

The French fleet, composed of 34 ships, has already divided up all the supplies brought by the last convoy from Europe: yet it still wants many essential things, especially powder and extra spars. The merchant convoy, bound to St. Domingo, sets sail at daybreak, under a special escort of two 50 gun ships. The fleet commanded by M. de Grasse then hoists sail, and by afternoon we were all at sea. The convoy sails to leeward of the fleet.

On the 9th at dawn, we saw the English and made out 49 sail. There reigned such supreme disorder among us at the time that the merchantmen were pellmell with the men of war, and we were afraid that the enemy would attack us in this confusion. All however was disentangled so well and so speedily that our line of battle was formed perfectly about 9, A. M., while the convoy, brought close together fell back on Guadaloupe.

This change of scene relieved our minds and kept the English in check. They, however, kept the weather-gage and came quite near us. At this juncture, a calm cut off their rear with half the centre from the rest of their fleet. M de Grasse then signalled to bear down and we had the advantage of cannonading the part of their fleet that could not be supported by the rest. This engagement lasted three hours and was indecisive, but it gave our convoy time to take refuge at Guadaloupe. Admiral Rodney by the help of a light breeze succeeded in bringing his fleet together, ran before the wind and insensibly disappeared from our eyes.

This action took place near the Isle des Saintes between Dominica and Guadaloupe. M de Grasse preserved the weather gage, but did not pursue the English, contenting himself with tacking in Dominica channel, and detached a frigate with orders, as we supposed, to get the convoy under way next night. This conjecture seemed to us the more probable, as it could while covered by us reach St Domingo without danger.

On the morning of the 10th the English again hove in sight. They seemed to have a regular move of tide by day and ebb at night and we kept on tacking in Dominica channel, holding the weather-gage.

On the 11th it was the same on the English side and ours. M. de Grasse's object in these manœuvres, which brought us up to the same spot, seemed to be to hold the English at bay to give his convoy time to reach St Domingo * * *

The sea in the gulf enclosed by these isles (Dominica, Guadaloupe, Marie Galante, Sainte) is ordinarily calmer than that without the same gulf. I saw it every night luminous in the ship's track, and the greatest heat that I observed up to this time was 22°, the least 10°.

It is not uncommon on this sea to see one vessel becalmed very near another keeping steadily on. This difference is always produced by a limited puff of wind, produced by some isolated cloud. These little currents of air which pierce the calm, and which mock the skill of commanders, sometimes decide the gain or loss of a battle. On the last occasion, for instance, when the English were separated and could not get together, had not de Grasse a fine chance, the whole French fleet having a wind? He had apparently good reasons for neglecting so considerable an advantage, which fortune proffered him

Although the action of the 9th was a small affair, yet it sufficed to give me some idea of a sea fight. Every one knows his post beforehand. A part of the crew remains on deck to work the ship and the rest are employed in the batteries; the cabin boys are engaged in furnishing the ammunition for each piece, and they fire as they get ready.

To say that perfect order then reigns in the vessel would be too much. The noise of the cannon, the cries of the boys, the gunners and the smoke, necessarily create some confusion in so small a space, yet it is not so great as to embarrass any one in doing his duty, it is rather a general hurrah that inflates the courage and increases the powers of each.

The English seem to fire in preference at the masts and we at the hull. Their method has the advantage over ours of disabling the vessels they engage sooner. Ours is more murderous, dismounts many cannon, and sometimes sinks a vessel.

The true reason of our different manner of aiming is perhaps that the timber of the English ships are less solid than ours.

Be that as it may, if the projects of this campaign are realized, the French will have more than one chance to cope with their enemies not only by sea but by land also

Seven thousand regular troops collected from all the Windward Isles, distributed in the vessels of the fleet and the convoy, are going to join 4,000 more French and 10,000 Spanish troops and 14 vessels of the same nation, which are at the cape. The most general opinion is, that we are going to besiege Kingston in order to take Jamaica from the English These are great preparations; beautiful projects! Shall we see them fulfilled?

April 12th. The dawn scarcely casts some light over the horizon, when we beheld our foe already ranged in good order; they approach us majestically The *Zélé*, one of M de Grasse's fleet, much injured by being run into, asks leave to put back, obtains it, and steers for Guadaloupe [1] The English at once try to cut her off M de Grasse, believing her in danger wishes to save her and signals his whole fleet to prepare for action and to bear down on the enemy.[2] Our vessels were then so dispersed, and their speed so various, that only nine were in line, including the flag ship about 7½, A. M, when we got near enough to engage.

The fire was very lively on both sides and so close that the grape shot alone pierced our second battery The English three deckers complaisantly presented their broadside to our smaller vessels so as to crush them more speedily.

For almost three hours the nine French vessels bore the brunt of the whole English fleet, when the *Glorieux*, 74, appeared like an isolated ponton in the midst of the field of battle, and drifting down on the enemy's line One of our frigates went to take her in tow, hoping to bring her to windward, within reach of help But the effort, praiseworthy as it was, was unsuccessful, and the officer in command of the *Glorieux* himself cut the tow-line so as not to compromise to no purpose one of our best frigates. Then hoisting the French flag on the stump of the main mast, he was seen in the midst

---

[1] The *Caton* had left us the day previous for the same reason

[2] Many sailors are of opinion that the *Zélé* ran no risk.

of the English with the utmost intrepidity firing both broadsides and receiving them on all sides.

But during all the time that elapsed from the commencement of the action, what were our other vessels doing? They bore down in succession, and as each got in reach fired separately, so that each had always several enemies on her. This inequality subsisted from the commencement of the action, and M. de Grasse in vain signalled them to rally; his signals were never executed. We lost the advantage of the wind about the middle of the day and some of our vessels were obliged to bear away. Others for the same reason kept so far to windward, that their presence became useless. At last at 3, P. M., the *Glorieux* being no longer supported and finding herself amid the English, struck after withstanding a terrible fire. Soon after the *Ardent*, *Hector*, and *Cesar* underwent the same fate. There now remained in reach of the English fleet only the *Ville de Paris* with a small number of our ships. The *Ville de Paris* in spite of her triple fire was soon surrounded and justly gave us the geatest alarm. Night was beginning to spread his sombre veil over that scene of horror and carnage, the starry heaven seemed to invite all nature to repose, but our infernal mouths still kept vomiting fire and death.[1] They at last ceased about 7½, P. M., and each one in our ship conjectured, without daring to say so, that the admiral himself had surrendered.

Till then we had kept the wind, a league from the English, but seeing Hood's division in pursuit of our scattered vessels, we ran before the wind and the darkness favored our retreat.

Had Commodore Hood sooner obtained of admiral Rodney the permission he solicited, as I have been told, to execute this manœuvre, in the disorder, distress, and consternation we

---

[1] The repeated commotions of the artillery made a calm succeed the breeze which prevailed during the early part of the day. Over a hundred thousand discharges of cannon were fired in this action on both sides, without including the fire of the swivels.

were all in, it is to be presumed that he would have found no great resistance in grappling several of our ships; while in fact they had time to escape, because he began the pursuit too late.

But we can say that we did not fight an instant in line. We gave ourselves isolated to the united English, who crushed our detached vessels by their superior number; and this manner of defeating us seemed so easy that had the day lasted a few hours more not one would have escaped. A terrible lesson for an admiral who neglects unity of action, on which all success depends. With a slight reflection on the manner in which the engagement was brought on, we must admire the fortune of the English admiral and be surprised that he profited so little by it.

About 9, P. M., our vessel was entirely separated from the rest of the French fleet. The captain commanding deems it proper to alter our course to the S. W., so as not to fall in with the enemy. We had scarcely made three leagues in this direction when a vessel hailed us. She was in our wake. We recognized one of our fleet and we agreed to keep company. The linstocks were kept lighted all night for fear of surprise, and each one stood to his post, but with no lights outside, to avoid being perceived.

About 11, P. M., we had, two or three leagues to leeward, the tragical spectacle of a vessel on fire. The explosion of the magazine was not long delayed, then the burning mass disappeared entirely. It was the *César*.[2]

On the 13th we endeavored to repair as well as we could do at sea, and we needed it greatly, for after the fight our sails and rigging were in rags, we had not a single sheet to the foremast. We had over eighty balls in the hull eight under the water line, and a hundred men killed or wounded of our crew of five hundred.

* * * * * * * * * * *

On the 9th of May, good day's sail, wind astern. In the

---

[2] It took fire in the hold in a barrel of ratafia which a drunken English sailor went to with an open lantern.

afternoon we see a man of war: we made signals; it was one of our frigates sent 'out from the cape to look for us; its mission being fulfilled it returns with us. The officer in command confirms the capture of M. de Grasse, which we had merely suspected; and informs us that the *Caton* and *Jason*, ships of the line, and the frigates *Aimable* and the little *Cérès* had been afterwards taken by Hood's division in the channel of Porto Rico.

---o---

Rodney's Account of the Actions of April 9th and 12th.

FORMIDABLE, at Sea, 14th April, 1782

Sir:—I must desire you will acquaint their lordships, that notwithstanding the disposition I have made of his Majesty's fleet under my command, which were stationed to windward of the French islands in a line stretching from the latitude of Deseada to the latitude of St. Vincent's, with a line of frigates to windward, which their lordships may perceive by the disposition of the fleet I have the honour to inclose, and which disposition was thought by every officer of the fleet to be such as to render it impossible for any convoy bound to the French Islands to escape, yet notwithstanding the vigilance of every captain and officer, the enemy found means to escape by making the island of Deseada, and creeping close under Guadaloupe and Dominique, they arrived safe in the bay of Fort Royal on the 20th and 21st of March

Information having been given me of this unlucky event, I thought it to be my duty to return to the bay of Gros Inlet, St Lucia, where I had ordered the store ships, victuallers, and trade bound to Jamaica to rendezvous

On my arrival in that bay every dispatch possible was made in refitting of the fleet, and taking in stores and provisions to five months of all species for the whole fleet: a watchful eye being kept the whole time on the French fleet in the bay of Fort Royal, as I knew that Counte de Grasse would hasten the refitting his fleet, and take the first opportunity of proceeding to the place of his destination

On the fifth of April, I received intelligence that the enemy were embarking their troops on board of their ships of war; and concluded they intended to sail in a very few days.

Capt Byron of the *Andromache*, an active, brisk and diligent officer, watched their motions with such attention, that on the 8th instant, at daylight, he made the signal of the enemy's coming out and standing to the northwest, I instantly made the signal to weigh, and having looked into the bays of Fort Royal and St Pierre's where no enemy's ships remained, I made the signal for a general chase, and before daylight came up with the enemy before Dominique, where both fleets were becalmed, and continued so for some time

The enemy first got the wind and stood for Guadaloupe; my van division under that gallant officer, Rear Admiral Sir Samuel Hood, received it next and stood after them. At nine the enemy began to cannonade my van, which was returned with the greatest briskness

The baffling winds under Dominique did not permit part of the centre division to get into action with the enemy's rear till half past eleven, and then only the ship next to me in the line of battle

Their lordships may easily imagine the mortification it must have been to the sixteen gallant officers commanding the ships of the rear, who could only be spectators of an action in which it was not in their power to join being detained in the calms under Dominique

The enemy's cannonade ceased upon my rear's approach, but not before they had done considerable damage to the ships of the van, and disabled the *Royal Oak* and the *Montagu*, and his Majesty had lost a gallant officer, viz: Capt Bayne of the *Alfred*, and a number of officers and seamen, but such was the steady behavior of Sir Samuel Hood and the ships of the van that the enemy received more damage than they occasioned

The night of the 9th the fleet lay to to repair their damages

The 10th they continued to turn to windward under easy sail, the enemys' fleet continuing to do the same, and always had it in their power to come to action, which they cautiously avoided, and rendered it impossible for me to force them, in the situation they were in between the Sainte and the Island of Dominique.

On the 11th of April, the enemy having gained considerably to windward, and the wind blowing a fresh and steady gale, I made the signal for a general chase to windward, which continued the whole day. Towards sunset some of the headmost ships of the fleet had approached near to one of the enemy's ships that had received damage in the late action, and had certainly taken her, if the Counte de Grasse had not borne down with his whole fleet for her protection, and which brought him so near, that I flattered myself he would give me an opportunity to engage him next day. With that view I threw out the signal for the form of sailing, and stood with the whole fleet to the southward till two o'clock in the morning and then tacked, and had the happiness at daylight to find my most sanguine desire was near being accomplished, by my having it in my power to force the enemy to battle. Not one moment was lost in putting it into execution, the consequence has been such as I have the honor to represent in my former letter of this day; and can say no more than that too much praise can not be given to the gallant officers and men of the fleet I had the honor to command. I have the honor to be, with great regard, Sir, your most obedient and

most humble servant,

G. B. RODNEY.

N. B. Lord Cranston and Capt. Byron relate, that the *Cæsar*, one of the captured ships, soon after she was taken possession of, took fire by accident and blew up, and a considerable number of people on board her unfortunately perished; and that Lord Robert Manners, died in his passage home in the *Andromache*.

FORMIDABLE, at Sea. April 14th, 1782

Sir:—It has pleased God, out of his Divine Providence, to grant to his majesty's arms a complete victory over the fleet of his enemy commanded by the Counte de Grasse, who is himself captured with the *Ville de Paris*, and four other ships of the fleet, besides one sunk in the action. This important victory was obtained the 12th instant after a battle which lasted with unremitting fury from seven in the morning until half past six in the evening, when the setting sun put an end to the contest. Both fleets have greatly suffered, but it is with the highest satisfaction I can assure their lordships that though the masts, sails, and riggings, and hulls of the British are damaged, yet the loss of men has been but small considering the length of the battle and the close action they so long sustained. The gallant behavior of the officers and men of the fleet I have the honour to command, has been such as must forever endear them to all lovers of their king and country.

The noble behavior of my second in command, Sir Samuel Hood, who in both actions most conspicuously exerted himself, demands my warmest encomiums; my third in command, Rear Admiral Drake, who with his division led the battle on the 12th instant, deserves the highest praise; nor less can be given to Commodore Affleck for his gallant behavior in leading the centre division. My own captain, Sir Charles Douglass, merits everything I can possibly say; his unremitted diligence and activity greatly eased me in the unavoidable fatigue of the day.

In short I want words to express how sensible I am of the meritorious conduct of all the captains, officers and men who had a share in this glorious victory obtained by their gallant exertions.

The enemy's whole army consisting of 5,500 men were on board their ships of war; the destruction among them must be prodigious, as for the greatest part of the action every gun told, and their Lordships may judge what havock must have been made when the *Formidable* fired near eight broadsides

Enclosed I have the honor to send for their inspection the British and French lines of battle with an account of the killed and wounded, and damages sustained by his Majesty's fleet

Lord Cranston who acted as one of the Captains of the *Formidable* during the action, and to whose gallant behavior I am much indebted, will have the honor of delivering these dispatches: to him I must refer their lordships for every minute particular they may wish to know, he being perfectly master of the whole transaction.

That the British flag may forever flourish in every quarter of the globe, is the most ardent wish of him who has the honor of being with great regard,

   Sir,

    Your most obedient humble servant,

      G. B RODNEY

PHILIP STEVENS, Esqr

INDEX.

Abercrombie, 43 n
Acadia, 51 n
Accaron, Antoinette Rosalie, wife of the Count de Grasse, 22
Accaron, Jean Augustin, 22
Ademval, Capt., 110
Affleck, Commodore, 109, 205
Aix la Chapelle, 32 n
Albert de Rions, d', 26, 50 n, 11 n; blockades Tobago, 47, 141, commands the Pluto, 111, 190
Albert, St Hippolyte d', 42, 43 n, escorts convoy to Europe, 86, 164
Alby, 128 n
Almon's *Remembrancer*, 45 n
Amblimont, Fuschembourg, Count d', 102, 113, 170
America and the Americans described by de Goussencourt, 88
Amherst, Lord, 44 n
Amoeneburg, 31 n.
Amphousse, Widow, 108,
Amsterdam, Journal printed at, 10
Anguilla, taken by de Bouille, 93
Andrews, History of the War, 33 n, 45 n
Anspach Troops, 80
Antigua, 100, 170
Antilles, 56
Anville, Duke d' 32 n
Arbuthnot, Adm., 29 n, 68 n, 138 n
Arnold Benedict, 138 n
Aros d'Argelos Capt., Baron d, 9, 26, 112, 123
Auxerre, 43 n
Azores, 182

Bahama Channel, 63
Balfour, Capt., 109.
Baltimore, 193, 73, 76
Baracao, 62
Barbadoes, 54, 95, 166
Barber, Capt., 109
Barclay, Capt., 110
Baredney, Capt., 110.

Barras, St Laurent, Louis, Count du, 71, 75, 77, sketch of, 67, joins de Grasse reluctant'y, 157 list of his squadron, 81; at Fort Royal, 95, at St Christopher's ib,, in action, 98; takes Monserrat, 105, 173
Barrington, Adm., engages d'Estaing, 16, 183
Basse, Terre, 95, 101, 166, 172
Bath 45 n
Battle of April 9, 114, 174, 197, plan, 117
Battle of April 12, 113, 120, 177; plan of 117
Battle between Arethusa and Belle Poule, 5
Battle between the Engageante and Rose, 16
Battle off Cape Henry, 158
Battle of the Chesapeake, 69-74. 151, 188 196
Battle of La Praya Bay, 33 n.
Battle of Martinique, 44, 111, 189, 193
Battle of St Christophers, 97, 99, 167, 169
Battle of Ushant, 15 20, 28, 101 n
Bay des Trepasses, 133
Bayne Capt, 109, 115
Bec du Raz 133
Behring's straits, 129 n
Bellisle 32 n
Bermuda, 16, 132
Bernadotte, 33 n
Biographie Bretonne, 43 n, Universelle, 44 n
Biron, Duke de, aids Rodney, 29 n
Blair, Capt., 109
Blanchelande, Philibert H R. de, sketch of, 144 n, at Tobago, 47 n, 145, 190 191
Bois de la Mothe, 28 n, 32 n
Bonite, 39.
Boscawen, Admiral, 28 n

Boston, 32 n, 44 n, 101 n.
Boubée, M de, his success, 62, 147; fêted at Cape François, ib.
Bougainville, Louis Antoine, Count de, 26; sketch of 43 n.; dispute at St. Pierre, 46; commands in battle of the Chesapeake, 104; in the Auguste, 113; retires to Curaçoa, 120
Bouillé, Francis Claude Amour, Marquis de, 38; sketch of, 38 n., attacks St Lucia, 46, 48, 143, 145, 190, takes Tobago, 49, 143, 145, 190; at Granada, 52; takes St Eustatia, 91, St Christophers, 102, 103; entertainments given by, 106.
Botany Bay, 129
Bowen, Capt , 110.
Breen's *St. Lucia*, 48 n.
Brest, 15, 20, 31, 33 n, 50 n, 55, 62, 129, 183, 165, 170, 189
Brevoort, J. C , has de Goussencourt's journal, 9.
Brimstone Hill, siege of, 96, 166-8, 169, 171.
Briqueville, Capt . 26.
Brun de Boade, Captain of the Réfléchi, killed 70, 105
Brunswick, Duke of, 30 n
Buckner, Capt , 109
Burgoyne, Gen , surrender of, 160, 196
Burnet, Capt . 110
Byng, Admiral, 32 n
Byron, action with d Estaing, 17, 33 n 101 n., commands the Andromache, 114, 202, 203

Caldwell, Capt., 110
Campbell, Col , 56 n.
Canton, Capt , 110
Cape Breton, 32 n , 51 n.
Cape Finisterre, 31
Cape Charles, 73,
Cape Henry, 74, 76, 88, 158, 164.
Cape of Good Hope, 33 n
Cape Pas · 55.
Cap François, 54, 56, 62, 85; description of, 57.
Captal de Buch, 19
Carenage Bay, 48 n
Caribs, 52
Carpenter's Rocks, 57

Castellane Majastre, Captain de 26, 111.
Castelnaudry, 101 n.
Castries, Charles Eugene Gabriel de la Croix, Marshal de, Minister of the navy, sketch of, 30 n.
Chabert, John Bernard, Marquis de, 26, 51; sketch of, 51 n ; saves the Diademe, 72
Chandos, Duke of, 28 n.
Charite, Capt de, 26, 111; offers to mortgage his plantations to enable de Grasse to go to the Chesapeake, 151
Charleston, 64
Charrington, Capt , 109.
Chas et Lebrun, *Histoire de la Revolution*, 28.
Chastellux, Chevalier, du, 76 n.
Cherbourg, 50.
Chesapeake, 63, 65, 73, 74, 113, 148, 149, 161.
Chilleau, Marquis du, 145, 146, 169, 191.
Choisy, M. de, reinforced by de Grasse's marines, 77, 195
Cibon, Christine Marie Delphine de. 28
Cicé, Champion de, 43.
Cicé Mgr de, Bishop of Auxerre, 43 n
Cicé, Monseigneur de, Archbishop of Bordeaux, 43 n
Clavel, Capt. de, 26, 113.
Clinton, Sir Henry, 66 n, 81, 86 n, 160.
Clostercamp, 30 n
Cockburne, Lt Col James, Gov of St. Eustatia, 93.
Columbus, 52 n
Compton, Lady Jane, 29 n
Conde, Prince de, 50
Congress, Resolutions complimenting de Grasse, 160.
Conway, Gen , 178
Cordova, Don Luis de, 33 n.
Cornwallis, Capt. William, 110, 113
Cornwallis, Lord, 66, 76, 77, 78-88, 149, 150, 153, 160, 161, 188, 195.
Corsica, 30 n., 46 n.
Courcy, Henry de, 9.
Courland Bay, 145, 191
Cranston, Capt. Lord, 204, 206

INDEX

Creoles, character of, 130.
Crosby, Capt , 110
Crossing the Line, 36.
Cuddalore, 33 n
Caraçoa, 120, 126
Custine, Adam Philip, Count de, 75.

Dalain, Capt , 26.
Dalins. Capt , 26, insubordination of, 56, appointed to the Neptune, 86, 113
Dames, Viscount de, 191
Damoy, Count de, 191
Daross, 9
Dead Chest Island, 55.
Descada, 202
Despinouse, Capt . 112
Destouches, Chevalier, engages Graves, 17, 84, 138 n
Décars, 26
Dety, Capt , 26, 112.
Dettingen, 30
Diamond Rock, 42, 141
Digby, Admiral, 140, 195
Dillon, Count, 191
Dillon, Capt , 129 n.
Dolphin, 39.
Domaines, 47
Dominica, 52, 121
Dominique, 202 204
Douglas, Capt Charles, 204
Drake, Rear Adm Sr Francis, 49, 71, 195, 205
Drake, Capt. Samuel, 109
Drayton, Mrs , 24.
Dufe d Orvault, 195
Dumaresq, Captain, 110
Duportail. Gen , 76 n
Dussieux, *Le Canada sous la Domination Française*, 44 n

Elk River, 195
Elphinstone captures La Touche Treville, 27.
Escars, Baron d', commands Glorieux, 26, 96, 112, killed, 122
Espinousse, Capt d , 26
Estaing, Charles Henry, Count d', 15, 63, 67 n ; outline of his campaign, 15-17, captures a vessel off Bermuda, 16 ; fails to blockade Howe, ib , baffled at Sandy Hook, ib ; operations in Rhode Island, 16 n , 32 n ; lets Hotham slip, 16 n ; engages Barrington, ib ; repulsed at St Lucia, ib , joined by Vaudreuil, 101 n., reduces St. Martin, 16 ; Granada, 17 n, 32 n , engages Byron, ib,; repulsed at Savannah, 17 n, 101 n., at Cadiz, 27, 29 ; satirical allusion to, 181.
Exchanges, none in America, 55.

Falkland Isles, 44 n
Fanshaw, Capt , 109
Ferguson, Major, capitulates at Tobago, 102
Flanders, 31 n.
Flechin, de, 100
Flyingfish, 40.
Fort Bourbon, 106.
Fort Nelson, 129 n.
Fort Prince of Wales, 129 n
Fort Royal, 17, 43, 44 n , 46, 47, 48 n , 51, 53, 54, de Grasse at, 46, 51, 54, 91, 94, 106 141, 116, 164, 165, 173, 189, inundated by waterspout, 54, Entertainments at, 54, 106; Fleet at, 202
Fort York, 129 n.
Fournier de Bellevue Lieut., killed, 100
Fox, Commodore, 28 n
Framont de, 43, 111 , captured, 126
Franklin, 41 n
Frazer, Sir Thomas, 96
Froissart, 19

Galeres, 40
Galvez, Senor, 129
Gardner, Capt. Alan, 109
Germain, Lord Geo , 150
Gazette de France, Extract from, 189
Généalogie de la maison de Grasse, 24
Genoa, 182
George II, 28 n
George III. 85.
Gibraltar, 29 n , 34
Gidoin, Capt , 109
Glandevèse Commander de, 26, 55, 90, 113, 142.
Gloucester, 76, 82 ; blockaded, 195, 196; surrender of, 78
Goimpy, Count du Maitz de, 56, 112

Goodall, Capt., 110.
Gordon, 100 n.
Goussencourt, Chevalier de, ineffectual attempt to identify, 9; hostile to Count de Grasse, ib; his Journal, 25, his description of the Americans, 87
Gouzillon, Captain de, 113.
Grasse, Alexandre Franç Aug. Count de, 23.
Grasse, Amelie R M de, 23.
Grasse, Adelaide, 23
Grasse, Francois de Grasse Rouville, Marquis de, 19.
Grasse, Francis Joseph Paul de Grasse-Rouville, Count de, biographical sketch of, 19; Captain of the Robuste, 20; at the battle of Ushant, 20; Commodore, ib ; joins d Estaing, ib , appointed to command of fleet, 27, 188; leaves Paris, 139; leaves Brest, 30, 189, writes to Rochambeau, 31 n, at Martinique, 41, 140, 189, engages Hood, 42, 140, 189, returns to Martinique, 46, 143, 190; sails to St Lucia with de Bouillé, 46, 145, 190, checked and retires, 48, 145, at Tobago, 50, 145; at Granada, 52, 146, at St Vincent 52, at Martinique, 54, 146, receives dispatches from U S, 148; difficulties, 149; sails to Chesapeake, 62, 152, takes Lord Rawdon, 73; at Lynn Haven Bay, 65, engages Graves, 69 74, 154-7; lands marines, 77, 158, sends de Barras to act in his place at the capitulation of Yorktown, 78, 84; defers to Washington's request, 85, 86 n, 102, sails back to West Indies, 88-90, takes St. Christophers, 96, 166, fights Hood, 97, 167, allows him to escape, 103, 168, defence of, 180; his fleet, 111; takes Monserrat, 163, 173, festivities, 100; engages Rodney, 114, 174, defeated and taken, 118, 120, 177, correspondence with Washington, 187-8; resolutions of Congress, 160

Grasse, Chevalier, Joseph de, at Louisbourg, 20.
Grasse, M∵ me de, 23.
Grasse Mélanie V. M. de, 23
Grasse, Sylvie de, daughter of Count de Grasse, marries M. Francis de Pau, 23.
Graves, Admiral, 71 n, 151 n; sketch of, 69; defeated by de Grasse, 69, 155, 194; his account of the action, 72 n, 73 n; Ward's opinion, 70 n., his loss, 73 n, de Goussencourt's opinion, 73, act'on with Destouches, 138
Greenwich Hospital, 29, 45 n
Grenada, 51, 54, reduced by d' Estaing, 17, 32 n; by Rodney, 27 n, Account of, 52; de Grasse at, 144, 146.
Grenadina, 54
Gros Islet Bay, 47, 143, 145, 190
Gundaloupe, 16, 197
Guérin, *Histoire Maritime*, 21, 70 n
Guichen Luc Urbain de Bouexic, Count de, sketch of, 28 n, succeeds d'Estaing 17, engages Rodney, 17, 20, 29 n, 101 n.; his fleet joins d'Estaing at Cadiz, 29; loses his convoy, 102
Hainaut, 31.
Hanover, 28 n
Havana 57.
Havre, 29 n
Hawke, Admiral, 28 n, 32 n, 101 n
Hennequin, 84 n
Hessian troops, 80
Heroism of a French sailor, 35
Hières, 182.
Historical Magazine, 56 n
Hood, Samuel Viscount, 44, 71 n, 151 n; sketch of, 44 n; engages de Grasse at St Christophers, 97, 167; escapes, 104, 108; in the Barfleur, 109; in the battle of the Chesapeake, 155, outwits de Grasse, 68 n, 99, 107, at de Grasse's defeat, 200.
Horseshoe, 86 n., 159, 195.
Hotham evades d'Estaing, 16
Houdon, 83 n.
Howe, Admiral, 16.
Hudson's Bay, 101 n.
Hughes, Admiral, 33 n

Iberville, 101 n.
Inglefield, Capt., 109
Inglis, Capt., 110.
Irish Brigade, 92 n.
Isle à Vache, 148
Isle de Groas, 132.
Isle aux Noix, 41 n.
Isle des Saintes, 197

Jamaica, 55, 101 n., 177, 178
James II, 92 n
James river, 74, 193, 195
Jaxton, Capt, 109
Jesuits, 67
Johnston, Commodore, 133 n

Kempenfeld, Adm., 28 n, 101 n
Keppel, Adm., 16, 179
Knedgett, Capt, 110
Knox, Gen, 76 n.

La Clocheterie, Chaudeau de, 15, 81, fights first battle of the war, 113 n, in de Ternay's fleet, 113 n; commands the Hercule, 113, killed, ib
Lafayette, Marquis de, 16, 63, 66, 75, 76, 151 n, 153, 189, 193
La Galissoniere, Marquis de, 32 n
Lagos, 32 n
La Grandiere, Charles Marie Count de, 81, 111
La Grange, 55
La Jaille, 128 n
Lake George, 43 n
Langara, Juan de, defeated by Rodney, 29 n
Langle, M de, 128 n
La Perouse, Jean François Galaup de, Sketch of, 128 n takes an English vessel, 27, commands expedition sent to Hudson's Bay, 101 n, 128
La Praya Bay, 33 n
La Touche Treville, Louis René de, sketch of, 27
La Vicomte, Capt, 112, killed, 123
La Villeon, de, 195
Le Begue, 9, 26, 111
Leeward Islands, 29 n
l'Estenduère, M de, 101 n
Le Moyne de Serigny, 101 n
Letendeur, M de, 28 n
Levarot, Count de, 191

Lemonade, 67.
Lincoln, General, 17
Linsec, Capt, 110
List of de Grasse's fleet, 26
Lloyd's neck, attack on, 68 n
London, 38 n, 43 n.
Lombard, M de, 84
Louis XVI, 38, 50 n
Louisbourg, 20, 28 n
Lutzelburg, 30
Lynn Haven, 65, 193, 195

Macarty, Capt Macteigue de, 111
McLauren, Capt John, 94 n
Madeira, 32
Maestricht, Siege of, 30 n
Malta, 32 n
Man-of war's bay, 115, 191
Manchineel, 53
Manners, Lord Robert, 110
Marie Galante, 129, 197
Marigny, Viscount Charles, 43 n
Marigny, Viscount, 26, 43 n, 84 112 killed, 123
Marmelade, 67
Martelly, Capt, 50, 113 saves his vessel, 124
Martinique, 38, 47, 165 171, 172 reduced by Rodney 29 n, de Grasse at 41, 42, 46, 84, 105; account of ladies of, 107 vessels at 128 action at, 42, 140, 167, 101 n, 144, 150
Matanzas, 64
Mathews Admiral, 28 n
Mattapony 156
Medine Capt, 111
Metz 7
Middlebank, 195
Middleground, 88 195
Mithon de Pencuilly, M de, 106, 112
Mogane Channel 171
Mole St Nicholas 61
Molly Capt 110
Monckton, Gen, 29 n
Monperon, Capt, de, 112
Monserrat taken by de Grasse, 68 n, 105, 167, 173
Montcalm, 43 n
Montclere, de 9, 26 112, 127
Monteil, Adhemar, Marquis de, 65, 97, 98 n, at Pensacola, 147 misconduct, 97

Monteil, Lt. Col. V. de, 55
Montluc. Capt , 26.
Morne Concorde, 190, 191
Morne Fortuné, 48, 143, 144, 190, 191
Morne de Vauclin, 41, 91.
Mornes, 41 n.

Nancy, 38
Napoleon, 28 n , 44 n.
Negapatam, 35 n
Negro Chasseurs, 191
Nelson, Admiral, 27 n
Nelson, Governor, 153 n
Nevis, surrenders, 68 n, 96, 97, 99, 103, 167, 168, 171
Newfoundland, 29 n , 51 n., 68 n, 132
Newport, 16, 32 n.
New York, 29 n , 81.
Notice biographique sur l'Amiral Comte de Grasse, 24
Northampton, Earl of, 29 n

O'Callaghan, *Colonial Documents*, 44 n
O'Conor, Capt , 92.
Orves, Count d', 33 n
Orvilliers, Count d', 15.
Ouessant, Battle of, 15, 20, 28, 101 n.

Pamunky river, 153.
Paris, 38 n , 51 n
Parry, Capt., 109.
Parker, Admiral, 178
Pau, Francis de, 23
Pau, Louis A de, 23
Pavillon, John François du Cheyron du, 120, 125
Penny, Capt , 109
Pensacola, Siege of, 55, 56 n , 147
Périgny, Lieut de, wounded, 190
Philadelphia, 148.
Pien, Catharien, wife of Amiral de Grasse, 22.
Pierrefeu, M de, 56.
Pigeon Island, battery on, 48.
Pilot fish, 39
Plessis, Pascault, du, 64, 183
Point Salines, 45 n . 140.
Port au Prince, reduced by La Touche, 27 , earthquake, 58
Point St Anne, 140
Portail, M du, 154

Porto Rico 55
Porto Cabello, 101 n
Portsmouth, 178.
Prescott, Genl , 100
Préville, Capt de, 26, 114, 120.
Providien, 33 n
Provence, 32 n , 33 n.
Quebec, 44 n.

Rappahannock, 158.
Rawdon, Lord, 78
Reduelas, Capt., 110.
Regiments, French:
  Agenois, 61, 100
  Armagnac, 191.
  Auxerrois, 47, 93, 191.
  Champagne, 47.
  Dillon, 47, 50, 92, 191
  Gatinois, 61, 85.
  Hainault, 102
  Irish brigade, 92 n.
  Lauzun's Legion, 61, 195
  Martinique, 47
  Royal Auvergne, 61, 63, 85.
  Royal Comtois, 192.
  Saintonge, 75
  Touraine, 61, 100.
  Viennois, 47, 191.
  Walsh, 92, 192.
Rennes, 43 n
Reynolds, Capt., 110.
Rhaal, Swedish officer, 195.
Rhidon, 97
Rhinberg, 30 n.
Robin, Abbé, 34 n
Roanoke, 55.
Rochambeau, Count de, 67 n , 76, 85, 198; reinforcements for, 84 n; letter of de Grasse to, ib; at Yorktown, 78, 84, 154; Resolutions of Congress, complimenting, 160
Rochefort, 27 n
Rodoard, Prince of Antibes 19.
Rodney, George Bridges, Lord, 65, 71 n, 151 n; sketch of, 28 n; early services, ib; engages de Guichen, 17, 20, 28, 55: attempts to recover St. Vincent, 29 n., seizes St. Eustatia, 29, 45, attempts to save Tobago, 50, list of his fleet, 109; watches de Grasse, 196; defeats him, 118, 120, 177; his account of action, 202

Rodney, Henry, 28 n
Rosback, 30 n
Rostaing, Major de, 128 n
Roussock, 153.
Ruyter, Admiral de, 179 n

Sadras, 38 n
Sainte, 204.
Sandy Hook, 16.
Sandy Point, 169.
Saumarez, Capt . 110.
Savage, Capt , 119
Savannah, Siege of, 17, 20, 33 n , 64, 101 n , 183
Scarborough taken, 191
Senegal 101 n.
Shark, 41
Ships, (American).
  Queen Charlotte, 76 n.
    (English):
  Agamemnon, 110
  Ajax, 73 n , 109
  Alcide, 110 , captures Hector, 123
  Alfred, 109, 115, 203.
  America, 109
  Andromache, 114, 164, 203
  Anson, 109
  Antelope, 44 n
  Arethusa 15
  Ariel, 128 n
  Arrogant, 109.
  Barfleur, 109, 123
  Bedford 109,
  Belliqueux, 110
  Bonetta, 81
  Canada, 110, 123
  Centaur, 45 n , 109, 142
  Charlotte, 187
  Charlestown, 128 n
  Charon, burnt, 67, 77
  Conqueror, 109
  Dublin, 28 n
  Duke, 69 n , 109, 125
  Eagle, 28 n
  Edgar, 71 n
  Fame, 109
  Formidable, 109, 206
  Fortunée, 72 n
  Gibraltar, 45 n
  Guadaloupe taken, 196
  Hector, 27.
  Hercules, 109
  Intrepid, 45 n , 73 n , 110, 142
  Invincible, 109
  Iris, 74, 158, 195.
  Isis, 27 n
  Jack, 129 n.
  Kent, 28 n
  London, 69 n
  Loyalist, 193.
  Ludlow Castle, 28 n
  Magnificent, 110
  Marlborough, 109
  Monarch, 110
  Montagu, 73 n , 110, 115, 203
  Namur, 28 n, 109.
  Nonsuch, 109
  Plymouth, 28 n
  Prince George, 28 n , 109.
  Prince William, 110.
  Princess, 81, 73 n., 109
  Prothee, 109
  Prudent, 110
  Repulse, 110
  Resolution, 109
  Richmond, 74, 158, 195.
  Robust, 110
  Rose, 16 45 n
  Royal Oak, 110, 115, 122 n., 203
  Royal Sovereign, 69 n.
  Ruby, 113 n.
  Russell, 45 n , 109, 123, 142.
  Sandwich, 173.
  Sheerness, 28 n , 69 n
  Shrewsbury, 45 n , 73 n , 110
  St Albans, 110
  Terrible, 69; burnt, 71, 73 n., 156, 195.
  Thetis lost, 48
  Torbay, 45 n, 109, 142 n.
  Triton, 94 n
  Valiant, 110.
  Warrior, 109
  Yarmouth, 109.
    (French)·
  Actionnaire, 55, 61
  Adour, 128 n
  Aigrette, 26, 193, takes a brig, 49, goes to Havana, 63, 152; brings in prizes, 67, 105, 154 , engages the Iris, 75, 158.
  Aimable, taken, 127, 202
  Alerte, 140
  Amazone, 128 n,
  Andromaque, 164
  Annibal, 32
  Ardent 84, 97, 113 123, 197, 200
  Arethusa, 101

Artesien, 20, 32.
Astrée, 100, 128 n.
Aurore, 26.
Astrolabe, 129.
Auguste, 26, 45 n, 113, 116, 128, 174, 194.
Belle Poule, 15, 43.
Bellone, 44 n.
Bourgogne, 26, 61, 69, 111
Boussole, 129
Brave, 102, 113, 127, 170
Cato, 43, 69, 70, 95, 111, 115, 127, 166, 194, 199, 202
Ceres, taken, 127, 202.
Cesar, 26, 43, 51, 112, 194; taken, 122, 200; burnt, 124, 201.
Charlotte, 187.
Citoyen, 26, 112, 194.
Concorde, 67; brings dispatches from United States, 148, returns, 152.
Conquerant, 84, 88, 94, 111, 128.
Constante, 148
Cormorant, 187.
Cornwallis, 91, 100, 102.
Couronne, 112, 123, 127, 173.
Dauphin Royal, 32 n., 112, 129
Dedaigneuse, 26
Destin, 55, 94, 96, 112, 125, 128, 194.
Diadème, 9, 26, 69, 71, 72, 73, 77, 95, 111, 125, 129, 193, 194.
Diligente, 26, 158, 193
Duc de Bourgogne, 84, 95, 109, 127.
Engageante, 16, 128 n
Eveille, 84, 112.
Experiment, 47, 49, 114, 129, 191.
Fantasque, 32 n
Fee, 61, 147
Fendant, 101 n.
Fier, 26, 54.
Glorieux, 26, 49, 50, 67, 75, 95, 96, 98, 112, 190, 191, dismasted and taken, 121, 122, founders, 126 n.
Guerrier, 44 n
Hector, 26, 27, 51, 54, 59, 61, 86, 89, 112, 167; taken, 123, 200, lost, 126 n
Hercule, 26, 113, 128, 194.
Hermione, 27
Heron, 32

Inconstante, destroyed, 60, 148
Indiscrete, 26
Intrepide, 56, 101 n ; destroyed, 59, 148.
Jason, 84, 112, 119; taken, 127, 202
Languedoc, 9, 26, 42, 97, 112, 123, 129, 194
Lion Brittanique, 95, lost, 96.
Magnanime, 9, 26, 112, 125, 129, 194.
Magnifique, 111, 127.
Marseillais, 26, 69, 101, 129, 185, 193.
Medée, 26, 51
Minautore, 26
Monarque, 32 n
Mouche, 26
Neptune, 84, 86, 97, 113
Northumberland, 26, 41, 62, 101 n, 113, 114.
Nourrice, 26.
Orphée, 32 n
Palmier, 55, 113, 114, 194
Pandour, 38, 41
Pluton, 26, 47, 49, 190, in action with Graves, 69, 111, 194.
Provence, 84, 86.
Reflechi, 43, 69, 70, 111, 115, 128, 193, 194
Resolu, 102
Richemont, 90, 102, 122
Robuste, 20.
Romulus, 17, 84
Rose, 16
Rossignole, 27
Sagittaire, 26, 34, 114, 129
Sensible, 26.
Sandwich, 187.
Sceptre, 26, 47, 95, 98, 112, 128, 183, 194
Scipion, 26, 113, 194.
Serapis, 190
Solitaire, 43, 94, 194
Souverain, 26, 43, 99, 113, 142, 194.
Sphynx, 20, 32
Surveillante, 164
St Esprit, 26, 47, 49, 50, 72, 113, 128, 194.
St Malo, 28 n.
Trident, 32 n
Triomphant, 101 n, 102, 109, 111, 120, 125, 183 n, 170, 173
Triton, 56, 70 n., 86, 164, 193

INDEX

Union, 26, 54.
Vaillant, 26, 86, 154, 193.
Vengeur, 32.
Victoire, 43, 86, 194.
Ville de Paris, 26, 31, 34; at Gros Islet, 48; strikes a rock, 147; in battle of Chesapeake, 69, 71, 104; Washington, on, 76, 158, 163, in action off St Christopher s, 98, 103, 112, taken, 123, 177, founders, 126 n.
Zele, 26, 33 n , 88, 95, 113, 116, 119, 174 n , 175, 176, 194, 199
(Spanish):
Phenix, 29 n
Shirley, Sir Thomas, 96.
Soulès *Troubles de l'Amerique Anglaise*, 85 n
Solano, Señor, 129
Spanish Town, 178
Sparks' Life and Writings of Washington, 34 n , 77 n
Splecum, Henrietta, 29 n
St Bartholomew reduced by d Estaing, 16
St. Cesar, Capt de, 113
St Christophers taken by de Grasse, 95, 96-103, 166-173 , described, 104, actions near, 166, 68 n , prizes taken at, 171
St Domingo, 55, 89, 178, 144 n , Account of, 58, Vessels at, 138, 147, 148, 150
St Eustatia, seized by Rodney, 29 n , 45, retaken by de Bouille, 91, 165 , garrisoned, 94, 95, 103
St. Goar, 30 n
St. John, Knights of, 32 n
St John of God, Hospitallers of, 57
St Lucia, d'Estaing repulsed at, 16, 183 , reduced by Rodney, 29 n , Hood, tries to enter, 45, de Grasse at, 41, 42, 46, 47, 144, 145, 191, Manchenillier, 63 ; English fleet at, 106, flag of truce from, 107.
St. Lucia Channel, 94, 95, 140, 166
St Malo, 44 n
St. Martin, reduced by d'Estaing, 16 , taken by de Bouille, 93.

St. Pierre, 46; entertainment given by merchants of, 108, 202.
St Simon, Marquis de, commands troops landed by de Grasse, 66, 154, 187, 188, 193
St. Vincent reduced by d'Estaing, 16, 178, 183; by Rodney, 29n ; de Grasse at, 52, 187, 196, 202
Suffren, Pierre André Bailly du, 33n., sketch of, 32 n.; in d' Estaing's fleet, 82 n., sent from Boston to Newport, ib.; blockades Savannah, 33 n., sails for East, 82 n , Bonbeo serves under 62.
Sullivan, Gen , in Rhode Island, 16
Sutherland, Capt , 110
Symonds, Thos , 83

Ternay, de, commands squadron, 17, 113 , dies of mortification, 18
Thompson, Capt C , 110
Thompson, Capt S , 110.
Thomson, Chas , 162
Tilly, M de, captures the Romulus, 17, in the Eveille, 84, 112
Tobago blockaded by de Rions, 47 ; de Grasse at, 48, 190, surrenders to de Bouille, 19, 190; description of, 50
Toulon, 15, 45 n , 51 n , 182
Tourville, M de, 63
Traversay, M de, 154
Trinquemale, 33 n.
Truscott, Capt . 109
Turpin, Capt , 26

Urville, M de, 129 n
Ushant, 15

Vanikoro, 129 n
Vaudreuil, Count de, 111
Vaudreuil, Lieut Gov of Canada, 44 n
Vaudreuil, Marquis de, 26, 101, 112 170, gallant conduct of, 114-5, 122
Vaudreuil, Marquis de, Governor of Canada, 101 n
Vilage, Capt de, 112
Villebrune, 84.

Viomesnil, Baron de, 105.
Virginia, 148.
Virgin Islands, 55.
Voyage d'un Suisse, 10, Extract from, 197.

Wallace, Capt Sir James, 109.
Walton upon Thames, 28 n.
Ward, Commander J. H , 70, 99, 121.
Waroquier, de, *Etat Général de la France*, 43 n., 92 n
Washington, George, 67 n., 75 n , 76, 153, 154; visits the Ville de Paris, 76, 158, 163, 195, forces Cornwallis to capitulate, 84 , correspondence with de Grasse, 187, remarks on death of de Grasse, 22; diary quoted, 76 n.
Waterspouts, 54, 90.
Wayne, General, 66 n., 153.
Wethersfield, 68 n.
Wilkins, Capt., 110.
William IV, in English fleet when Prince William, 85
Williams, Capt , 109.
Williamsburg, 193, 195
Windward Isles, 38, 104, 129, 164.
Wolfenbuttel, 31 n.

York river, 73
Yorktown,, 68 n , 76, 82, 153, 161, 196

CPSIA information can be obtained at www.ICGtesting.com
Printed in the USA
LVOW09s1018201214

419745LV00008B/257/P